WEST CHURCH OF THE NAZARENE
REV. DALE CRALL, Pastor

1313 Bristol, N.W.
Grand Rapids, Mich. 49504

This Adventure Called Marriage

This Adventure Called

MARRIAGE

by

MILO L. ARNOLD

BEACON HILL PRESS ● *Kansas City, Missouri*

Dedication

To Eva on our thirty-sixth wedding anniversary

We count them o'er today, our string of pearls,
  Three dozen years since you and I were wed;
A rosary of living, each year a jewel,
  A gem of loving on a silken thread.

The God of love has blessed our marriage pledges;
  His present vigil has been always near.
He touched with light the distant jagged ridges,
  And made a landscape of the things we'd feared.

The loveliness of many frosted winters,
  The fragrance of as many summer flowers,
The nectar of a million sweet caresses
  Have made this jeweled necklace fully ours.

Adown the years we've wept and feared together,
  And each has known the lonely touch of pain;
Yet, counting back along the string of pearls,
  We see where love has found the greater gain.

And so today we thread another jewel
  Upon the slowly lengthened strand of time,
And pray that hand in hand throughout the seasons
  Our love may make this pearl the most sublime.

                                        MILO

Foreword

This volume originated in the hot crucible of human experience rather than in the cold test tubes of science. It is made up of the somewhat irregular and unusual bits of truth molten from years of sharing this human adventure. It is the laughter and songs of happy homes captured and passed along that you too might enjoy them. It is also the gathered moans, sobs, and tears which have accumulated at the author's desk as the long parade of people paused one by one that we might pray and weep over the shards of their broken dreams. They are the mingled residue of golden success and ashen failures, sorted from the lives of people over a period of three dozen years in the warm fellowship of the pastorate.

In this we do not pass on to you any tasty morsels of gossip nor betray in any wise the confidences shared in the privacy of ministerial counsel. These belong only to the person sharing them and the ears into which they were willingly whispered. Here is only the unidentifiable distillation of the nectar of joy and sorrow emanating from the human experiences and condensed into lessons for living.

Actually this volume is a gift to you from the hearts of those who have succeeded and those who have failed, those who have wept and those who have laughed in the swaying battle of being a human in a desperately big world. They allow me to pass it on to you with their good wishes for your success in the exciting adventure we call marriage.

—MILO L. ARNOLD

Contents

For this cause shall a man leave his father and mother, and shall be joined unto his wife, and they two shall be one flesh.

—Eph. 5:31

CHAPTER ONE

Putting One and One Together

What a move! A young man and a young woman whose lives have been quite unrelated are moving together. Their personal belongings, their accumulated relics, their clothing, their whole estate, so intimately their own, are being brought together, exposed to each other and becoming their mutual possessions.

All his life he has had a room of his own in the home of his parents. In this room everything was his and in this room he belonged to himself. Here he lived with his thoughts, his music, his dreams, and his wondering. Through her entire life her room has been her personal domain. In it she laughed and cried, dreamed and primped. It was a little world where she could be alone with her treasured possessions, her secrets, and her moods. Here she lived under the guidance and surveillance of her parents. They had been responsible for her subsistence, her protection, her clothing, and her happiness. It had been a personal world so intimate that only her diary could share it with her.

Now they have met and loved. They have found so much in common that they feel themselves mutually indispensable. They are ready to dare take each other's hands and share each other's fate for better or for worse till death shall part them. They have gotten the legal consent of the civil authorities, the blessing of their friends, and their vows have been made at the altar of the church. Now the time has come for a move. What a move! How charged the emotions, with hopes and fears, timidity and boldness, eagerness and reserve! They are in the process of putting one and one together.

There is his trip to his parental home for his "things." His clothes must be carried out of the old house while Mother looks on with mixed emotions. His hi-fi, his tennis racket, his school mementos, his books, and all the possessions which are his. Some of his boyhood belongings suddenly seem too childish and they are thrown out or given to some younger brother. There is the trip to her home to get all her things. Clothes, odd pieces of light furniture, mirrors, cosmetics, books, and all the accumulation of trinkets and gimmicks which fill her closet and bedroom to the brim.

Heretofore they both had their own rooms, their own clothes closets, dressers, and space, but now they meet to store them all in one room. They look at the closet and decide which end shall be his and which hers. Of course, in time it will be mostly hers, but at the starting point it is supposed to be half and half! They divide the dresser drawers for his things and hers. They arrange the odd pieces of furniture, the pictures, and the whatnots, not as his or hers but as *theirs*. They put up the curtains, stack their dishes, and enjoy the adventure of a lifetime.

Following the honeymoon the task appears hopeless for a time, what with all the wedding gifts to unpack, to place, and to move about until they are fitted into the pattern of utility and attractiveness. Her wedding gown is to be stored and the half-burned candles to be boxed for future use when they eat by candlelight. Suddenly the house is very full of their things rather than his things and her things. It is full of the makings of a home.

It is not hard to move possessions together, for they will fit into most any house or apartment. It is not hard for them to move their mailing addresses to the new home, for a little time and thoughtfulness will soon establish their "Mr. and Mrs." address. It does not take long for them to move their material and physical assets together, but the matter of moving their lives together is a different project. It is pleasant and exciting but it takes longer, for the person is not all moved at one time nor can it be packaged neatly for transport, in either a parcel or a van.

The articles each contributes to the house are of little import compared to the persons they contribute to the marriage. Even their lithe, youthful physiques and attractive faces are not the total persons. The real discovery of what is involved in the marriage awaits more deliberate discovery.

Furniture, clothing, pictures, and even physical appearance are all made of quite well-defined standard patterns and can be fitted together very quickly in conformity to the demands of cohabitation. Personalities, however, are different. Each personality moves in a world of its own. It is the product of every experience, every influence, every lesson, every injury, and every adventure of its total past. The resulting person is different from any other person on earth.

The chief contribution brought to a marriage by each partner is not something hung in a closet, nailed to a wall, or stood in a corner. It is not something put in a joint account in the bank. When all these things have been settled, given and taken, then the two persons must begin honestly to face their marriage with the actual persons they are. Now there is nothing to shield them, nothing behind which to hide, nothing to decorate what is ugly nor to camouflage what is shameful. When the real experience of living together starts, then the real persons who are doing the living must come to the fore and be seen, undecorated and without veneer.

The person—that is it! The person is what is married. Not things the person owns, what he looks like or feels like, but the person as he or she exists in the honesty of total exposure to reality!

Marriage is God's idea. In all His creation He has seen fit to guarantee some social aspects. He so made us that our lives would need the completeness which is supplied by a partner of the opposite sex. None is altogether self-contained. There is a sense in which no one can find complete fulfillment apart from marriage. In the beginning, though man companioned even with God himself, the Creator knew man's need for one of his own kind which would be bone of his bone and flesh of his flesh. This companionship would provide for one of the finest human qualities and the richest culture of life. Though some have degraded marriage to the level of mere legalized prostitution, the fact still remains that God's plan was lofty. Humans need marriage, not merely for procreation, but for enrichment of life.

14

In the situation of marriage both lives are given a chance to flower. Here maturity can reach a finer quality. Life is given a fuller meaning, a broader dimension, and a divine purpose. Of no other human association has God said that it is symbolic of the relation between Christ and the Church. Marriage can, however, become a very unhappy situation. Many of the tears that are shed are the result of unhappiness and disappointment within marriages. This is of all suffering the most painful and of all sorrow the most bitter. A happy marriage in a very poor cottage is to be chosen rather than an unhealthy marriage in an expensive home.

Marriage is a blessed state or a dismal state, depending upon how the two persons involved are related to each other. In this study we will not deal so much with the selection of a mate as with guidance for those who have already made their irrevocable choice. There is much more to marriage than merely giving two people the same name and mailing address.

Moving two persons into the same house does not make them one. Getting married does not fuse two personalities. It is true that they become one flesh in that they are mutually indispensable to each other in the fulfillment of life's purposes, but their distinct differences persist. Defining the bounds of liberty within the framework of the bonds of matrimony is our project. Actually it is the differences which make marriage exciting and adventuresome.

The marriage must not be allowed to completely submerge either person. It must not create a situation where one is seriously dominated or suppressed. It must not be allowed to imprison or suffocate either personality. Personalities must breathe and be free. They must have room. They must have rights and liberties and opportunities for self-expression. The two persons must be put together in such a way that each can stand tall, enjoy individuality, self-fulfillment, and adventure. Many marriages become desperately unhappy when one party is dominated by the other. This won't work and soon festering irritation will result.

Each marriage partner must have areas of domain. He must have spheres where he makes decisions and she must have areas where the decision is for her to make. He must have rights but so must she have rights. Neither of them must be made afraid of the other nor live in apprehension of what the other will say and do. Some men seem to think it necessary to keep their wives afraid of them, and some women rather enjoy keeping their husbands always on edge for fear of being slashed by a berating tongue. Whatever sense of authority such domination produces will be short-lived. One and one cannot be put together in this way without resultant heartache for both.

In a marriage each partner should be treated as a person with rights—rights to money and friends, to enjoy pleasures and to make decisions. Each has physical rights which the other should respect. Each must reverence the other in such a manner that these rights will be gladly, naturally, and effectively granted. One and one are two people, and two they must be kept and as two they must live. Neither of them dares become either an extension of or a property of the other. It is neither necessary nor desirable that they always agree, nor that they completely enjoy the same things. It is necessary, however, that they respect each other whether or not they agree.

THE CONTENT OF A MARRIAGE

Putting One and One Together Is Basically for the Purpose of Fulfillment Rather than Mere Happiness. Sometimes two people are considered happy together because they settle for the same small contentment. Their marriage is placidly happy but it does not cause either of them to aspire or climb. Immediately after marriage they settle down to merely enjoy each other. They get what help they can get from kindly relatives. They work when they must and soon take what jobs they can get. Eventually they find a berth on welfare rolls and contentedly live in their poor shack, surrounded by pets, poverty, and poor neighbors. They adjust their aspirations to their situations and conform to their small world. Here they chat and laugh, loaf, wake, sleep, and ruminate at the expense of the taxpayers. Their marriage may be happy in its way but it has not been entirely effective.

Effective marriages should kindle noble aspirations in both marriage partners and in every child born into the home. Sometimes people with drive get on each other's nerves but this is a lesser hazard than indolence. Better it is to be stimulated to higher service, more adequate living, and more lofty selfhood. A good marriage should be basically happy but it needs a great deal more to it than happiness. An effective marriage needs challenges, enlarging responsibilities, and dreams. There must be about it a kind of constant discontent which will not allow either person to stop learning and developing as long as life remains. When two people marry they must adjust to each other, but they must never try to become merely happy at the cost of personality growth.

When One and One Are Put Together They Must Be Able to Communicate. This is one of the most difficult areas in many marriages. A man and woman may both speak the English language, both be able to read and write, and both be gifted speakers and writers, and still be unable to communicate with one another as they should. Communication in marriage is the bridge between two personalities. Only what they can communicate of themselves becomes truly their area of meeting.

17

Their marriage unites no wider portion of their personalities than their communication permits.

Most persons potentially have a great deal more to give to their marriage than they do because their abilities to communicate are limited. Sometimes people love more deeply than they can express effectively. Sometimes they do more fearing, yearning, suffering, and hoping than they are able to reveal to their mates.

Communication is always an uncompleted project. No two persons ever become completely acquainted. As long as they live, they continue to discover new personality areas as their communication is enhanced. Even golden wedding couples can testify to new areas of interest discovered. Together those new discoveries are explored bit by bit.

The Past Is Part of the Person. The young person approaching marriage thinks in terms of life as it was experienced in the home of his or her parents. The patterns of behavior and the emotional climate in which a person has grown from infancy become the norm for the person unless for some definite reason the person chooses to rebel against them and make a change.

In some homes people scream at each other while in others they speak with great courtesy. In some homes things are thrown in heaps, scattered in wild confusion, or left to clutter any spot where they were last used. In others they are all provided a place and kept there. In some homes children are taught promptness, orderliness, and punctuality while in others the clock is robbed of all authority.

When the two persons being united in marriage are from radically different home patterns, they will find their adjustment difficult. It will be a real advantage if they will carefully adjust their lives upward to the level of the best prepared partner rather than allowing it to gravitate to the behavior pattern of the less cultured one. To do this they will need to use firm self-discipline and loving patience in making their adjustment. These differences are often minimized during courtship but rise to assert themselves under the persistent pressure that comes when living together.

Married persons do not live together as the persons they wish they were nor as the persons they try to make others think they are. They become, openly and without disguise, their true selves with all the imperfections as well as the ideals.

Unless a person is capable of being at home in a situation very different from that of his or her parental home, the adjustment can be difficult indeed. The parental home leaves definite personality identifications which may vary so much in the two persons who marry as to demand radical restructuring of both conduct and attitude.

Here the miracle of divine grace and the empowerment of the divine presence is the catalyst needed. When two persons seek sincerely to become like Christ, they will rapidly become like each other in those things which are basic to happy marriage.

Accumulated Sex Ideas Are Part of the Persons Too. Possibly the most frequent difficulty encountered arises from the different backgrounds in their thinking about sex and its place in life. Family backgrounds differ widely here and create almost incompatible attitudes in a very intimate life exposure. In the home where one marriage partner was reared, the subject may have been dealt with wisely and frankly without the least stigma being attached to it. In the other home the opposite may have been true. The subject was never mentioned in the home; if questions were asked, they were quashed and the child came to associate the matter with the naughty and vulgar.

Some parents intentionally paint sex as a very bad thing, thinking to protect their child from personal sins and from the bad intentions of others. Most often this unrealistic concept is given to little girls, who become deeply impressed by it. Teaching done during early childhood cannot be easily forgotten. Many such children are so inhibited that they have very abnormal courtships or marry with very limited courtship experience. With such a background of training the mere expedient of a marriage ceremony will not change the person's concept of sex from one of vileness to one of purity.

Sometimes both marriage partners are equally inhibited and the result is a limited enjoyment of marriage, even though it is not infected with bitterness or misery. However, if the backgrounds are quite opposite at this point it is going to be difficult to arrive at a mutually satisfactory relationship. Both must make an effort to understand and adjust, or frustration on the one hand and repugnance on the other will result. These attitudes of inhibition change slowly and sometimes revert quickly to their original status under pressure. There must be a readiness to learn, to explore, and to improve the situation by unselfish yielding on the part of both persons.

Men often fail to understand the deep aesthetic sensitivity of their wives. The result is that some well-intentioned and genuinely good men are thought to be beasts while some very devoted wives are blamed for being uncaring and selfish. Many tears are shed in secret by good people who want to be adequate partners and find it exceedingly difficult to move one and one together in a happy marital relationship. Often both are devout Christians, both pray sincerely about their mutual problem and strive to find a better relationship, but many have to settle for a less-than-satisfying way of life.

The counsel of a careful and understanding pastor can be of great help in lifting the matter from the area of guilt to the place it should occupy. So long as the matter of sex is treated as something base, it will be a source of trouble. When both persons discover the loftiness of the physical relationship as a trust from God and a capacity and privilege to be used in partnership with Him, then there is the possibility for the individuals to find a common meeting ground.

Putting One and One Together Includes Appearance. When two people who are unusually good-looking marry, or when two who are unusually homely are mated, some problems are avoided that occur when opposites in this respect are joined. While love may be blind to the difference, the world is not so blind. The one who is less good-looking is in danger of becoming jealous, suspicious, and insecure. It is not likely that the goodlooking one will tire of the other, but the other is likely to suffer from the poor comparison he or she makes in his or her own mind or of which one may be reminded of by some crude outsider. The one who feels inferior will become suspiciously vigilant lest the mate show any lack of personal attention or lest some other person might receive some unusual notice.

Family Backgrounds Are Part of Putting One and One Together. Sometimes people meet at the railroad tracks and forget that one comes from one side and the other from the other side. Sometimes one comes from a home of poverty and the other from a home of affluence. Sometimes one comes from an unknown family and the other from a prominent one. Sometimes one comes from a family where some members are in disrepute while the other family is highly respected. Love is not blind when it sees the good in these widely divergent people and there is no reason why they cannot be happily and profitably married, but there are difficulties which they must face and solve.

Both persons in such a combination must be magnanimous. Both must learn to respect the other and the other's family and include the relatives in their affections and homelife. They must not allow either side of the family to monopolize them nor deprive them of fellowship with the other side. Nor should they allow parental influence to deprive them of their responsibility to live their own lives. Nor yet should they ruthlessly cut ties and hurt feelings. It is often better for young couples from such varied home situations to move to another community and not invite the relatives to move along. They need not be a long distance away, but they need to be where they will not have to bear stigmas nor be required to live up to reputations for the sake of relatives. They should be in a position to make their own way, erect their own image, and become known for the persons they are.

When One and One Are Put Together, Their Likes and Dislikes Must Adjust. If one liked spinach and the other did not like it before they were married, the wedding ceremony won't make them both like it. If one liked music and the other didn't or one liked picnics and the other hated them, the wedding won't change a thing. If one has many personal likes and dislikes and the other has a host of conflicting likes and dislikes, they had better do some reconciling and adjusting before the wedding—or call the whole thing off. If either of them is so immature as to be unwilling to change, there is trouble pending. There is no excuse for any husband being hard to cook for or repeatedly sabotaging his wife's dinner plans because he doesn't like certain foods. He should love his wife and respect himself so much that he would learn to like it or else swallow it and brag on it if it chokes him. By the same token, if there are things he likes and she does not, she should be big enough to learn some new likes. Why should both lives be forced to live within the narrow confines of a whole list of insistent dislikes and notions imposed by either one? Some couples have little room left for living by the time they move back from all their immature notions.

These adjustments must all be made without loss of selfhood or dignity on the part of either person. Individuals cannot be forced into shape by another. They must voluntarily work out a personality contour compatible with the mate whom they love so sincerely. When love has been destroyed, the adaptation becomes extremely difficult and differences are inclined to increase. So long as two people sincerely love one another there is every reason to think that they can reconcile these personality differences.

Sometimes Previous Marriages Must Be Accepted Facts in a Marriage. This may be difficult. If one has been previously married and the other has not, there is a different set of problems than when both are coming to marriage for the first time. Sometimes the one who has been previously married feels in possession of more knowledge and experience and hence attempts to take too much lead. While the past experience may truly provide some education, the person so experienced must realize that the past was with an entirely different mate and thus the entire marriage situation has a different dimension. Every person is an amateur in every new marriage, for putting one and one together requires new initial adjustments with this new marriage partner.

Another possible residue of a former marriage experience is the tendency to make comparisons. If the former marriage was happy, the remarrying person is tempted to compare the new mate with the old or to expect the dreams and hopes of the former home to be fulfilled in the new one. Sometimes the deceased partner's virtues are magnified while the faults are forgotten.

By the same token, the mate without a previous marriage may fear being compared or otherwise associated with the phantom which lingers of the former marriage partner whose place has been entered.

Persons remarrying after the death of a former mate are much better risks than persons whose former marriage ended in divorce. Death leaves a clean wound which heals without a scar. Divorce leaves a scar and often a lingering infection. There is no bitterness associated with death such as is invariably related to divorce and separation. The success rate for remarriages of divorced people is much less satisfactory than that of first marriages.

SEX AND MARRIAGE

Prenuptial Sex Behavior Will Attend the Wedding. One and one can be put together more effectively if it is not only the first marriage for both, but if it is the first sex intimacy for both. If a person finds in marriage his or her only sex adventure, it is much easier for that person to associate all sex wistfulness with the legitimate marriage partner. Furthermore, this is the only ground upon which the marriage mate can trust a person. If virtue has been guarded and disciplined throughout life, how much better the foundation for marriage!

When two people are joined in marriage after they have indulged mutually in sexual intercourse premaritally, they find lingering problems resulting from their unchastity. In the first place, the liberties they have taken with each other tend to make them so indispensable to each other that they are drawn into marriage either prematurely or unadvisedly. In the second place, they both respect themselves and their mates less and bring to their marriage a bit of tarnish. Through their lifetimes they bear a gnawing sense of guilt. This sense of guilt often asserts itself in the times when they should enjoy each other most. Something lovely is taken away.

24

There is a sharp relationship between divorce and the premarital unchastity or delinquency of the parties involved. This is in part due to the fact that persons whose lack of self-discipline allows them to indulge in things they know are not right will also be lacking in self-discipline when they are married. Persons who lack the willpower to discipline themselves during their later teen years will not receive an automatic power for self-government by the magic of the wedding ceremony. They will remain in marriage the kind of persons they were prior to marriage, and persons lacking in self-control make poor marriage risks.

The relationship one makes between premarital behavior and marital success reflects also his basic attitude toward sex expression. Is this part of life strictly physical and sensory or is it a reverent communication of selves? Is it a mere body demand or is it a divine trust? Is it a meaningless plaything or a meaningful yielding of spirit as well as body to one we deeply love and to whom we have given our entire selves? Promiscuity before marriage indicates a strictly physical estimation. If the spiritual factors were considered, people would treat it reverently and protect it by the framework of the law of God and society. Persons who give a totally physical dimension to such a spiritually and morally involved experience indicate that they have not the capacity for knowing or cherishing things above the level of the flesh. The physical drive is in command and this bespeaks problems in the involved relationship of marriage which must endure for the remainder of their lives. People who willfully commit a spiritual sin for the sake of a physical sensation are not indicating their readiness for weighing the values involved in making a marriage and a home succeed.

We have no firm figures on the number of marriages in which the bride is already pregnant. Such figures cannot be safely compiled due to the absence of dependable records. Estimates based on the best information available would indicate that one in every five or six is pregnant. This is a frightening figure. This is a serious situation, both socially, morally, and spiritually. If this number of conceptions occur, we can be sure that a much larger number of people have been morally lacking in self-control. The number of young men coming to marriage after having discarded chastity is obviously greater than the number of women. Yet the moral and emotional qualities of a young man are as vitally important to making a home as are those of the woman. Chastity is always golden.

Unfortunately some otherwise very fine young people from good homes are victims of their own lack of discipline and bear their first child embarrassingly soon after their marriage date. An alarmingly high percentage of these marriages fail within a few years. Fortunately, some are sufficiently mature to rise to their new responsibilities and make good. It remains true, however, that a painful percent of the couples whose marriages decay or become unsatisfying in later years are persons who were premaritally pregnant.

When a couple discovers that their undisciplined desires have gotten them into this embarrassing situation, they should do some very deliberate thinking. They will do well to go to their parents and to their pastor for the benefit of mature judgment in picking their course. They cannot bypass their moral responsibility. They are old enough to have known and done better. They have violated a law of God and a law of society. They have injured themselves and all who love them. They must accept this responsibility and do all in their power to minimize the damage caused.

If they are qualified for marriage and can rise to the occasion, they should marry and provide a name and a home for their child. If they are adequate, even though young, they can learn to love each other and can with discipline and maturity rise to live effective lives. We would not discourage their marriage, provided they have the basic qualities essential for success in making a home. They will, however, do well to seek the counsel of trained professional help in making the right emotional and mental adjustment.

A major factor in their success must be their sense of divine forgiveness. The inner guilt must be forgiven. Sin is sin, and they have sinned grievously. While the sting of guilt remains they will be lastingly prisoners of it. They will never rise above it by merely calling it weakness, a mistake, or an accident. They must confess that it is sin and find the forgiveness of God and the forgiveness of each other if they are to deal effectively with this situation. Marrying to cover a sin does not deliver them from it. The sin must be confessed and forgiven. How fortunate are all humans that God does in His mercy forgive sins!

The high failure rate of marriages in this group is not altogether due to the permature pregnancy but can in part be traced to the fact that the people who become pregnant before marriage are often the people who have other emotional and social problems. These problems are not solved by marriage and usually tend to grow into larger issues through the years. Another factor is the youthfulness of many of these marriages. A frighteningly large percent of the pregnant brides are high school girls or girls just out of high school; many are only junior high school pupils. They are too young for marriage; they are not sufficiently mature for the responsibilities they must accept; and the immaturity is often more a factor in the marriage failure than at first appears. Physically, both male and female mature rapidly, while emotions, attitudes, and judgment develop more slowly. When the eager, ready body is not under command of a mature and prepared mind, not only will people get themselves into problems before marriage, but they will continue to make for themselves problems if they get married.

The effects of illegitimately premature conception is often obvious in later life when the physical drives of both should still be eager and wholesome. The terrific emotional shock inflicted upon the girl who finds herself in trouble before marriage leaves a deep mark. Nor does the boy escape. They are simply overcome with fear. They think of suicide, of running away, of ruined lives and every terrible thing. When the fact dawns upon them that they will be found out, that they will hurt their parents, their friends, and their own lives, there is an inevitable association between the sense of guilt and the sex experience which brought it about. Many times this impression of guilt will be lastingly associated with their sex lives. Fear, shame, and humiliation cast long shadows over their total marriage span. This may contribute, even much later in life, to incompatibility. Some people far down in the sunset years, sorting through their memories, are still bearing the full painful impact of the ordeal of premarital sexual relationships.

Putting one and one together is God's idea and it can be made to work perfectly. It is just what we need for the fulfillment of our own lives and the ennobling of our total selves. God planned it, originated it, and looking upon His work said, "It is good." Marriage is wonderful, but we humans need to remember, in this area of life as well as in others, that though God provides us with the resources we need, it is up to us to discipline ourselves in the use and adaptation of His blessings.

The courtship practices of many couples are responsible for inhibitions of their marriage. If when they were dating and engaging in the various common activities by which young people become acquainted they had kept their areas of interest lofty, their marriage would have profited. If they had worshiped together and developed a mutuality of spiritual communion, it would pay big dividends throughout the years. If they had engaged in wholesome recreation and activity together, they might have enlarged their common interests broadly. If they had enjoyed intellectual exercises, discussed ideas, philosophies, and concepts, they might have discovered not only personal but mutual adventure. If they had sought to broaden their base of understanding rather than merely enjoying being together, their forthcoming marriage would have benefited.

Too many courtships are basically only a process by which two people become better acquainted with each other's pleasures and passions, and provide no occasion for knowing each other's deeper spiritual aspirations, needs, or interests.

By this we do not mean that dating should be prudish, chaperoned, and stiff. Dating must be gay, informal, playful, and impetuous, but if it includes the broader range of experiences and acquaintanceships, it will provide a better indication of whether or not marriage is desirable.

Going to church together before marriage will give important clues to the religious adjustments which will need to be made. Going to the library together may give insight into the patterns of philosophy and sociology which each has. Going to concerts together may reveal the aesthetic tastes which will become important in a marriage. Visiting in each other's homes will give indications of the background differences which will rise up later on. Praying together will help two people find that deep spiritual rapport which is essential to full acquaintance and communication.

Of course dating will include recreational activities, parties, fun, and frivolity. It will include time together in privacy and the trifling nonsense and chitchat which go with venturing more and more intimately into each other's lives. All this is part of a growing acquaintance, but if it degenerates into a mere series of petting parties and lovers' lane experiences, it is no longer true courtship. When it becomes only an orgy of lust and physical sensations, it ceases to be courtship and blinds the involved persons to the basic truths which surround them. They are then hurried unseeing into a marriage which has only an accidental chance at success.

How fortunate are the Christian, the cultured, and the mature young people who make their courtship and dating a part of their real preparation for marriage! They include God and wonder, reverence, and respect in their approach to the marriage altar. They have become acquainted with the broader circumference of each other's lives and personalities. They can enter marriage with prudence and preparation.

Marriage includes the total person. The courting and acquaintance by which people decide whether or not they are suited to be married to each other should include the broader interests in life. If the bodies, the minds, the spirits, the cultures, and the attitudes of the people must marry and live together, it is certainly unwise to ask only the bodies if marriage is to be entered into.

Persons who find that they have entered marriage at the strong urging of the flesh, with too little else in common, will do well to set about immediately to establish these broader areas of communication. They should set out with a purpose to find a rewarding religious life. They should establish a family prayer and worship pattern. They should be dedicated Christians and jointly include the church, the family devotional activities, and the community responsibilities in their program for life. They should systematically further their education and their cultural appreciations. By the grace of God individuals are capable of self-change, and improvement becomes an exciting possibility.

*The husband must give the wife what
is due to her and the wife equally
must give the husband his due. The
wife cannot claim her body as her own;
it is her husband's. Equally, the
husband cannot claim his body as his
own, it is his wife's.*
I CORINTHIANS 7:3-4
"New English Bible"*

CHAPTER TWO

Selfishness and Orange Blossoms

Selfishness Will Not Homogenize. It is not soluble
in a social situation and will not lose its shape when
placed in even the most softening climate. There can be
no place so warm as to melt it, no solution so permeative
as to shape it, and no blow so violent as to break it.
A selfish person does not change shape or nature. Only
after the selfishness is removed does the person become
ductable, pliable, or adaptable. If two persons are to
come together in marriage successfully, they must be
sufficiently plastic that their lives will shape to each
other smoothly and comfortably.

Selfish persons are never comfortable when in close proximity to another individual, for they do not want to conform to the likes, desires, interests, and wills of others. They resent any situation which requires an adjustment of their own convenience. They want to find happiness by getting other people to do all of the conforming, and it is utterly impossible for one member of a marriage pair to conform sufficiently to compensate for a nonconforming mate.

A self-centered person cannot be truly happy, yet happiness is required in the intimate social relationship of a marriage. Happy marriages are made only of happy persons. Unhappy marriages are the result of unhappy persons being married. When a selfish person marries, there will inevitably be a price to pay. The marriage may last; it may have a limited kind of happiness and may appear entirely wholesome before the world, but there are heights of enjoyment to which it cannot possibly reach.

Many times marriages which appear at first to be utterly happy will find the orange blossoms withering to droopy dejection when the two persons come down off their cloud sufficiently to discover the monster of selfishness hiding among their marriage possessions. What a disappointment when the ugly head of self-centeredness lifts itself among the lovely accumulation of experiences which adorned the wedding season! Selfishness is always ugly, but when it gets into a home where love is, there is nothing so difficult or unbecoming.

Sometimes selfish people get married. In fact, they are often more eager for marriage than are the unselfish ones, for they see in it an opportunity for security, for attention, for pleasure, or for personal aggrandizement. They see in it an opportunity for individual benefit. Selfish persons may well want a mate. Their wants are intense and eager and they will cover their hook of selfishness with utmost care in order that they may lure the most promising mate to their grasp. In fact, they can cover their nature of greed so well that their prey does not have the slightest indication of being snared until it is too late to do anything about it. Selfish people marry because they want to *get* a good mate rather than because they want to *give* or be one. They want to *get* a home rather than wanting to *make* a home. They want to *get* love rather than yearning to *give* love in all its outgoing wholesomeness. Once they get a marriage partner, they discover that they are still unhappy and begin to blame their mate for not making them happy. They will ask more and more from them, wringing from marriage every drop of service and devotion they can get while continually giving less and less.

Most marital unhappiness can be traced in one way or another to selfishness. Of course, the selfish person does not acknowledge the fact and will stoutly say that the selfishness is all on the other side; but, acknowledged or not, it is there with all the deadliness of a plague.

Selfishness Is Basically Immaturity. A baby is utterly self-centered. When a baby wants to eat, it makes no difference how inconvenient the time is for its mother or father or for the whole family. He does not hesitate in the least to disrupt the entire household for what he wants when he wants it. Here we use the masculine pronoun for convenience only, for little girls are as given to selfishness as are little boys. No baby cares a thing about the comfort, the sleep, the desires, or the convenience of anybody else on earth. A baby wants what he wants when he wants it, and that is that.

This way of looking out for number one is quite acceptable in an infant, for how else would infants survive in such a selfish world? Only by making themselves heard, making themselves irritating and unnerving to others, can they get their needs cared for. Sometimes, however, a person gets to actually enjoying the benefits of this kind of one-sided concern and tries to carry the licenses of babyhood over into the years beyond infancy.

We know that the baby is maturing when he begins to think of the wants and needs of others. He is growing up when he begins to wait until morning to yell for something rather than to disturb the household. When he begins to find enjoyment in seeing other people happy, he is maturing.

Jesus was of all persons on earth the most completely mature. He lived entirely for others and gave no thought to self. He said, "It is more blessed to give than to receive." He meant it, too, for He lived that way. He said the way to find your life is to lose it, and the way to lose it is to seek to keep it for selfish purposes. He was utterly unselfish. He was not in the least contaminated with greed nor inclined to self-pity. He found His pleasure in serving, His joy in giving, and His success in saving others even though He could not save himself while doing it.

If this is maturity, then there are many immature people in the world; and if immaturity and selfishness are related, then there is need for a lot more growing up in our generation and our society.

Selfish Persons Often Marry at an even younger age than others, because they see in marriage an escape from personal responsibilities. They think that if they marry they can escape the mandates of their parents—the authority of their fathers or the instructions given by their mothers. They resent the demands that are made upon them by family members; hence they want to marry and get away from it all. How terribly mistaken they are, for down the line they will find that marriage is for mature people! It is for people who will become servants of persons they love. It is for people who will be willing to give for the joy of giving and serve for the honor of serving. It is for people who will take care of selfish babies and help them learn to be unselfish. It is for people who will work long hours for others and be glad to do it, doing without things that others might have them, and still find pleasure thereby.

Sometimes people who know they are classified by their friends and relatives as being immature seek through marriage to take a sudden step to loftier social status. They seem to feel that getting married and becoming their own boss will automatically make them into adults. They overlook the fact that adulthood is a state rather than a status and is gained only by what they become, rather than by what they do. So long as infantile, childish, self-centered attitudes remain in the person, there is no possible election or situation which will grace him with adulthood.

When people grow tall and wear adult clothes, yet still "want what they want when they want it" regardless of the convenience of others, they are only children in overgrown bodies. They are only playing at being adults. So long as men and women say what they think without regard to the feelings of others they are immature, selfish, and childish. Whenever a person tells all he knows, cannot keep a confidence, and cannot be trusted with a secret, he is being childish and should not except adult confidence.

Some very strapping men think not a thing of being rude and unkind to their wives. They seem to think they are such big boys that it is smart to be a bit rude and bossy. Like spoiled little boys, they want to show off like men. Really mature men won't be unkind to anybody, especially to the folks who love them and whom they profess to love.

Some very beautiful women dress in fine clothes and display many social graces when they are in public and are trying to impress their neighbors, but when they are at home they snap and snarl, pick and nag, fuss and whine like little girls arguing over lollipops. The trouble is that they are selfish. They are immature. They don't care how deeply they hurt the people who love them or how much they disappoint the folks who have to put up with them. Such grown girls might possibly make acceptable P.T.A. presidents but they make very unsatisfactory wives and mothers. Selfish people don't make good mates. Strong homes, like strong houses, are made of mature materials.

Falling in love does not make people unselfish. Children who love their parents are still selfish with their parents until they eventually are helped to mature into a way of life which centers around others and around God rather than around self. A man and woman can genuinely love each other and still one or both of them be extremely selfish. It is very possible for immature people to love but their love is not fully rewarding, fully enjoyable, and fully meaningful. Love, such as is needed for happy marriage, must be a mature, unselfish, wholesome kind of love. Selfishness is inimical to everything worthwhile in marriage.

Selfish people are emotionally unstable, socially unpredictable, and spiritually insecure. Their emotional and spiritual fortunes rise and fall with every chance wind of fate which blows against them. They are quick to think they are being abused and very slow to see that they are abusing others. They lack a full scope of interests because they are too concerned with self and personal pleasures. They are likely to take little joy in the loveliness of the world around them, for they are too wrapped up in things they possess or can consume upon themselves.

They like to dominate situations as much as they can, be it at home or away. It makes them feel important to be able to control other lives. They usually find fault with the way other people do things. Seldom

can another person do something so well as not to be
criticized by them in one way or another, particularly if
it is an area in which they have some personal skill.

A self-centered husband will almost invariably find
something derogatory to say about any other man or
any other man's work if his wife should mention the
other man kindly. A selfish woman will seek to defend
her own stature by cutting down every competitor to
attention or praise.

With these attitudes in a marriage, jealousy and
suspicion are inevitable. No home can be truly successful when blighted by these beasts of prey. We don't
want to just "stay married," but we want to have happy,
effective homes. God intended that marriage be a true
adventure for us. It should meet needs which are basic
in us. It should be as comfortable and as pleasant as the
relationship between Christ and His Church.

How to Conquer Selfishness

The first step in overcoming selfishness in the
home is the same as the first step in dealing with anything sinful; that is, *Confess It.* Be honest about it now:
Are you acting immature and childish? Are you wanting your own way simply because it is your way rather
than because you can prove that it is best? Are you
saying things that hurt your companion which you
would not say to respected people outside the home?
Are you expecting privileges without being ready to
extend privileges?

When company is in the house or when you are in
the presence of friends, do you sometimes try to make
yourself look good by embarrassing your mate? Do
you tell things which seem to you to be a good joke on
your husband or wife which you would not want him to
tell if it was on you? Do you like to tell about his
mistakes, blunders, or foolish sayings which make him
appear juvenile and by doing so give you the personal

pleasure of appearing superior? This is a poor way to snatch recognition, for while your mate may have blundered in doing it, you are being selfish and immature by telling it for your own pleasure. Furthermore, relating such tales sometimes boomerangs—to your own embarrassment. Joking is fine and laughter, mirth, and hilarity should have some place in all our lives; but when it is indulged in at the cost of mutual trust between marriage partners it is dangerous.

When your companion dents a car fender, do you call it carelessness while calling the same thing an unavoidable accident when you do it yourself? When your mate spends money on some article which is worthless, do you treat it differently than when you do it? When your mate allows a high-pressure salesman to get the name on the dotted line, do you make a scene about it while expecting him or her to be utterly understanding when you make one of those unwise "investments"? If we treat the situation differently when our mates are at fault than when we are responsible, it is a symptom of selfishness and immaturity. Children do it that way, you know. It is always easy for us to rationalize our own foolish acts, but it takes a mature person to try as hard to brush off the unwise acts of another.

Are you able to distinguish between *wants* and *needs* when your personal desires are involved, as easily as when your spouse desires something? Sometimes our own wants become needs much more easily than the wants of other people. An unselfish person will be inclined to be generous with the other at this point.

Since the immature, selfish person is by nature governed more by physical desires than is the unselfish one, the more a situation is related to the flesh, the more poignantly selfishness expresses itself. Without a doubt many marriages suffer their most serious injury when selfishness expresses itself in the physical, more intimate conjugal relationships. These intimate physical expressions must be enjoyed by both persons if they are to be lastingly enjoyed by either. The person who selfishly demands a physical using of the other person is being most immature. Personal desires must have relevance to the wants, wishes, and desires of one's mate. Any person who is old enough for marriage ought to be mature enough to respect the intimate personal rights of a companion. This goes for both husbands and wives, and if either of them is selfish with regard to this connubial responsibility and privilege, the cost will be high. Marriage is for mature people. People are not qualified for satisfactory mating merely because they are eighteen or twenty-eight or forty-eight. Chronological age has little to do with emotional maturity after a person is physically grown.

Many couples who appear quite congenial in public are beset by selfishness day after bitter day when they are at home and the curtains are drawn. It is true that wives often manifest no concern for the emotional and physical problems of their husbands, while on the other hand countless men are as selfish as beasts with regard to their wives.

Maturity and unselfishness progress as we learn to be honest with ourselves, to discipline ourselves, and to see others as well as ourselves in a true light. Maturity is the ability to hold self responsible and to make it mind. It is the ability to blame self sensibly and do something about it. It is the capacity to be aware of the feelings and intentions of others and to place the best possible construction upon what they do and say. The Apostle Paul, in writing the thirteenth chapter of his first letter to the Corinthian church, gave one of the finest papers on maturity which has ever been penned. Maturity is the quality that is able to love unselfishly. How relevant this is to marriage!

Selfishness Affects the Health of the People as Well

as the Health of the Marriage. Parents can teach children to be selfish just by letting them enjoy special benefits from having their own way. For example, if a child learns that by being sick he gets special attention, he is likely to feign sickness just to get waited on, to get his own way in the arguments with other children, to be excused from doing things he dislikes doing, and to escape unpleasant duties. He revels in the attention and cuddling, special diets, and favored chairs in the house. He enjoys being talked about, pitied, and honored. This may be all right for a really sick child, but usually the less parade parents can make over the illness of a child, the better. If the child learns to capitalize on the illness, it may be that he or she will continue to do so. Many people have practiced their illness until it has become a profitable way to live and they lack the courage to overcome it.

Woe betide the person who grows to marriageable age having learned this "art" of living! Such a person, falling in love, will suddenly be in the best health he or she has ever known. Everyone looking on is thrilled with the excellent "recovery" and the fine chance the couple have for marriage. This is very good—as far as it goes. But there is usually trouble down the line. The time will come that there will be the same kind of burdens and responsibilities in the new home as existed in the old one and there is almost sure to be a return to the same old escape mechanism. The selfish person may get sick and get sick often, stay sick long and drain every possible bit of attention and pity from the experience. Selfish people try to get attention and have their way by getting sick. They expect to be immune to blame and responsibility because they are suffering so much. Many people have been invalids for life even though there is nothing organically wrong simply because they have found in sickness a sounding board for their self-centeredness. Not all selfish people become invalids but some do and when it happens they become a major burden upon their mates and their children.

Unselfish people get sick too but they do not pity themselves, make a parade of their sickness, nor seek attention by reason of it. Children can grow up in a home where sickness is a constant guest without becoming marked badly by it provided the sick person is unselfish. It may even help them to cultivate a spirit of sympathy and compassion. Not so when the sickness is induced by selfishness.

Orange Blossoms Never Wilt if They Are Kept in a Climate of Unselfishness. The orange blossoms from the bridal veil are as fresh for the silver wedding, the golden wedding, and the funeral spray as they were for the wedding night if they are preserved daily in the fresh water of sincere unselfishness.

Homes graced by unselfish mates produce unselfish children. Unselfish mates enjoy living together and their unselfish children are pleasant to live with. Selfish people never create happy homes nor rear completely happy children in their homes. Selfish people are always snatching. They speak unkindly, they blame others, and are irritated by the people who share their rights in the household.

Did you ever go into a home where there were selfishness, quarreling, complaining, and faultfinding? Did you ever listen while parents quarreled with their children and with one another? Did you ever see a home where everybody felt cheated and robbed? The members of the family were cheated and robbed! They were robbed by selfishness, the meanest thief in the whole world. What selfishness takes away from a home cannot be brought back nor can what it destroys be rebuilt. New things may be built over the ruins but that which was destroyed is gone.

41

Jesus Christ tried so earnestly to teach us to live unselfishly! Over and over again He emphasized it, but we are so slow to grasp the truth! Even Christians can find it a hard assignment. It should be so easy when basically unselfish in its nature.

Marriage Requires Nothing Which Is Not Basic in All of Living. The person who is adequate for life is adequate for marriage. Marriage requires no qualities or characteristics which are not basic to the Christian life. It is just that under the close relationships of marriage the inadequate persons show up more readily. When people are really ready for life they need not be afraid of marriage and its responsibilities. Humans are made for marriage, and God ordained marriage for humans. It is normal for people who are mature, and should be entered into as a God-given privilege.

Marriage and the Christian Life Are Related. This does not mean that all Christians have happy homes, for they do not. Neither does it mean that all people who are not Christians have unhappy homes. It simply means that everything that is involved in being a Christian is basically involved in the making of a successful marriage. The more truly Christian persons are, the more adequately they can live as marriage partners. The more Christian persons are, the more wholesomely they mature. If persons who profess to be Christians are unable to live happily together, it is obvious that they are missing some qualities of the truly Christian life. If they can but apply these Christian graces to their lives more fully, this will be reflected in increased marital happiness.

Nothing could so reshape the climate of many homes as a genuine commitment of the marriage partners to God. No person can genuinely consecrate himself to God without yielding up his selfishness. Christ taught us how to become adequate persons. His specific rule was crucifixion of self. There is no other way for marriage to fulfill its divinely appointed purpose.

Only an unselfish heart can enjoy the open avenues of communication with the people and things about. Selfishness imprisons the person within the small world of personal interest. As long as a marriage partner keeps a significant area of life closed to the other member, there will be suspicion, hardship, and unhappiness. A self-centered person will inevitably keep that closed area, for the defensive nature will avoid any total exposure of oneself to another.

Legend tells of a man purported to have died and been taken by an angel to see heaven and hell. He was first taken to hell, where, to his utter surprise, he saw people sitting, long-faced and utterly miserable, at long tables loaded with choice viands and every delectable dish. At first he could see no reason for the misery which attended their silent contemplation of the food. However he soon noticed that they were supplied with knives, forks, and spoons with handles four feet long and none of them could hold them in such a manner as to feed himself. The result was that they were all starving while seated at a loaded table.

He was then carried to heaven and to his amazement saw similar long tables with similar food and similar knives, forks, and spoons but the people were having an absolutely hilarious good time, for they were feeding each other across the table. Not only were they well-fed but they were getting acquainted; they were having an adventure and communicating their fun to one another. Of course this is but a legend, but it does give us a hint of truth. Marriage is like that. It is heaven or hell, depending upon whether we sit and mope for what we want and can't get or whether we find the adventure of giving others what we cannot directly get ourselves. The result of the latter is that we will find others feeding it back to us. If all the

43

husbands and wives who sit across tables from each other would figuratively get excited about feeding each other, they would find much happiness. So long as they sit gloomily contemplating their own wants and pitying themselves for their own inconveniences they will make their homes a place of torment for themselves and those who live with them.

Let's have some fun in life! Why not grab that long-handled spoon and start doing all you can to make your mate happy? You cannot bring happiness to yourself until you bring it to your household. You cannot enjoy your blessings alone nor think first of self and find any meaningful reason for living. Jesus was so right, "He that loseth his life . . . shall find it." "It is more blessed to give than to receive."

We must be realistic and face the fact that some unselfish people, unfortunately married to selfish mates, may be unable by unselfish living to accomplish a reform. They hopelessly pour themselves into an insatiable vortex until after years of giving and living they are faced by the cold, hard fact that they are accomplishing nothing.

Some selfish mates will be impressed by no language but the threat of divorce. When they think they are going to lose their mates they begin to get concerned, not because they are reformed, but because their interests are to be served best by a show of penitence. The usual result is that the divorce action is dropped, after which they return to their impositions, continually going just as far as they think it possible without losing their long-suffering mates. There is no outside cure for selfishness. The change must take place within the individual himself, and that by the transforming grace of God. Even the long-outlawed public whipping post where recalcitrant characters were publicly flogged would not make a person grow up.

I have seen long-suffering, gracious, and basically unselfish little wives with their faces beaten to a pulp repeatedly, their clothes ragged, their bodies emaciated and underfed, who have poured their whole selves out in a hopeless effort to make a home. What advice can you give in such situations? We often wish that the mother and father who reared such a self-centered scoundrel could have forseen the price a wife and children would pay because they did not make their child mind, did not make him respect others, and did not make him do some growing up during formative years. If boys are allowed to plunder the rights and privileges of others at will without ever learning the responsibilities of being a social person, they will not change after marriage. Parents who do not require their child to live unselfishly in its childhood home are inflicting a terrible price on the man or woman that child will someday marry. Getting older will not of itself mature the child emotionally. The school, the church, the neighborhood society of children and adults, and the laws of the land will try to fill in where parents fail. But others cannot undo the cultivated selfishness which is instilled in a child by being always allowed to have his own way in the home. The kind of person he is at home is the kind of person he will be in his own home after marriage. The trouble is that by that time he will not break toys but hearts and not scratch furniture but personalities and souls.

Selfish people cannot be good husbands, wives, or parents; so the people who marry them and are born of them will suffer for it and may likely pass on to the next generation the injury which was done them. Fortunately, the grace of God and the miracle of becoming a true Christian can enable a peron to reverse this attitude and pattern of selfishness.

Selfishness is a condition not easily overcome. It is basic to the original, sinful nature of man. It is the essence of the carnal nature. It cannot be easily forsaken nor cultivated away. Herein we need the loving grace of God. He alone can cleanse and purify the heart of man and free him from bondage to himself. He who merely fights it in himself or picks at it in a spouse will be unsuccessful in effecting a remedy. He who commits his way utterly to God in total commitment, and by faith permits the atonement of Christ to be fully effective, will enjoy this freedom which is freedom indeed.

Not only would marriages be enriched but the persons involved would find life splendidly enlarged and freed by seeking and finding that miracle of the divine ministry in the human situation. Only as self is crucified with Christ can love flower in its full, glorious fragrance.

And Isaac brought her into his mother Sarah's tent, and took Rebekah, and she became his wife; and he loved her: and Isaac was comforted after his mother's death.
—GENESIS 24:67

CHAPTER THREE

Marriage Wears Clothes and Lives in a House

A Marriage Cannot Live in a Goldfish Bowl. Marriage is such an intimate, personal institution that it must clothe itself becomingly and enclose itself within walls. People living in the frigid north would be unable to endure the cold were it not for the fact that they dress for it and enclose a small area of space which they can heat to a comfortable temperature. So with marriage. The wide society of earth is big and cold. A marriage must find some spot which it calls home, must condition that separated bit of climate to suit its needs, and must clothe itself with such qualities as make for health.

47

Houses can be purchased or built and may be large or small, ornate or simple, but the home which is enclosed in them must be individually produced by the people who are united there. A family is that group of people—two or more—who are ensconced together in the bonds of a home. The home is the product of the total experience of togetherness. Ardent romancing may lead up to and result in a marriage of two people, but the making of a home requires much more than romancing. People can have a very exciting courtship and, following marriage, move into a very desirable house, and still create an utterly intolerable home.

Most of the experiences in a home are quite humdrum. In fact, most of life is as unglamorous as turning off the light at night and turning off the alarm clock in the morning. Most of the time in the home is consumed with the sameness of daily chores and the regularity of routine. No marriage needs a home where excitement is constant nor a situation where there is a lot of time for play. A wholesome marriage needs a situation where there is work but where people do it together. Work done together by people who are in love is genuinely exciting. Even the most masculine boy can find it absolutely exciting to dry dishes provided the pretty neighbor girl is washing them. Tasks which are boring of themselves can become uniquely pleasant when done as part of the coquetry of love. Homes do not need less work but more love. If the hard work of a home is wedging the marriage apart, there is something wrong.

Every marriage must move into a house in order to make a home, but it is the privacy of walls rather than the dimension of rooms which is essential. The personality quality which the persons give to the home is more relevant than the convenient largess provided by material accoutrements. Of course, facilities too crowded or too inadequate can work a hardship on a home; but since people who love each other can live in less space than those who do not, we find it more important to have largeness of heart than of house. The actual clothing of a marriage includes the habits, the attitudes, the aspirations, and the behavior patterns of the persons involved.

Homes are less injured by the hardships visited upon them from without than by the infections and irritations arising within. No home can close its doors against adversity and hardship. No symbol or fetish can be placed above the door which will frighten away lurking disease or death. No insurance will protect against bereavement, sorrow, and tears. No walls are secure against misunderstanding, human error, and physical or social loneliness which surrounds us in the world, and only those who keep a candle of love burning brightly will avoid the gloom which comes to the solitary.

The secret of a good home is in accepting the inevitable, acknowledging human limitations, embracing the days as they come, and making the best of what life brings. We dare not allow these things to burden the household overmuch. We must learn to use them, to master them, and to sharpen our own lives against their rough edges. No family needs immunity from the demands of hardship nor escape from the disciplines of pain. Homes need rather the genius of love which will accept these situations as a challenge and a call to greater maturity.

Since families are constituted of persons, it is obvious that the dimensions and qualities of the home cannot be greater than that of the individual personalities. The first step in enriching a home must be taken through enriching the persons involved in it. Even small-souled people can want a happy, adequate marriage but only those who are mature enough to discipline themselves will possess it. Meaningful marriages are not the product of a ceremony but of a lifetime of mutual self-cultivation. Inadequate persons will be frustrated when trying to clothe a marriage and home with suitable loveliness.

A Good Climate Is Essential to a Growing Marriage Relationship. A husband and wife must live in a climate as surely as they live in a house. And they choose and create the climate as surely as they do the house. That climate is created by everything they are, everything they do, and everything with which they are associated. It is made of attitudes, things, sounds, people, and clothes. It is shaped by memory and hope, by yesterday and tomorrow.

God and a religious faith are essential to the finest climate. No home climate can reach its absolute best without the awareness of God and the constant love of God being expressed in the daily living situation.

When the Christian religion reaches the benighted pagan lands, the most obvious change is wrought in the marriage pattern of the people. Women cease to be bought and sold like cattle. Babies begin to be loved and wanted. Little girls become as welcome as are little boys. Marriages begin to be limited to one mate, and love begins to be a determining factor in choosing that companion.

Today the vitally Christian marriages enjoy a very high success rate, while the homes where God is left out suffer much more serious attrition. The finest guarantee for a marriage is a genuine Christlikeness in the lives of the partners. Christian faith and godly living create a climate which produces the loveliest flowering of the lives and the home.

Persons contemplating marriage should give serious thought to their ability to enjoy a congenial religious climate. Radically different religious backgrounds can be desperately hard to hurdle. At the time of marriage they appear quite simple but under the strain of daily living they are not lightly set aside.

If one partner has been reared in a climate of liturgy and form while the other has spent the most formative years exposed to informality and freedom in religion, they should discover a wholesome meeting ground before they marry. If one is Catholic and the other is Protestant, there will be serious problems. If one keeps Sunday and the other keeps Saturday, or if one eats meat and the other has scruples against it, there will be difficult adjustments to make. If one takes religion very seriously and the other is merely casually religious, or if one is a Christian and the other is not, there is cause for grave concern if they proceed to marry.

Before the engagement these things should be carefully weighed, and before the marriage a definite plan should be made. A church should be chosen, a family religious pattern designed, and a Christian climate produced for the nurture of their marriage. Care should be taken that basic convictions are not taken lightly and that the adjustments are in peripheral things rather than basic matters. No person should marry at the cost of his or her soul. No person should expect another to marry at such a cost. Our religious adventure is more important than our marriage adventure and it is better to walk a single path with God than a double path without Him.

A marriage needs a church, not only for the wedding ceremony but for the enrichment and ennobling of the everyday experiences. Every couple need friends such as are found in church. They need the cultural exposure which is provided by active participation in worship and service to God. In a relationship so involved and sacred as marriage, people need a personal sense of the love and fellowship of God in their individual lives which will communicate to the marriage.

THE FINEST HOMES ARE UNFINISHED HOMES

A wedding is completed when the minister hands over the signed document and the state recognizes a couple as legally married. A house is eventually finished when the last nail is driven and the last painting done. A marriage, however, is never finished. A marriage placed in a home must be a perpetually changing, living, growing thing. It never remains static for two consecutive days. If its growth becomes arrested there is no way to prevent decay. People who comprise the marriage must increase in stature proportionate to the needs of its growing pattern or they will become inadequate. Married persons must be capable of personality growth because their situation of living is inevitably one of change and new demands.

A couple must be prepared to change when the first child is on the way and particularly when it is born. A home is utterly overhauled by the arrival of a baby, and parents who are not qualified to adjust to this enlarged demand will be frustrated indeed. Following this not only the parents but the child must be taught to change as other babies arrive. No two babies arrive in the same kind of home, even though they are born to the same parents in the same house. The first child comes to a hitherto childless home and effects the radical occupation of the place. The second child comes into a home where an older brother or sister has broken the first path but has already arrived and is there first with most. The first child arrives to find a new layette, new crib, and newly wondering parents. The second comes to a marriage where having babies is not an entirely new experience. The parents must be capable of changing sufficiently to give each child an adequate and equal opportunity, even though no two can be given the same situation. Though the parents must be distributed more ways and give less individual time to each of many children, yet the later children coming to a home amid well-chewed toys, rickety high chairs, squeaky playpens, and worn carpets can still have a very abundant life if the home climate is conducive to happy living. In fact, children arriving to join already sizable families have many advantages.

Homes change, not only with the arrival of each new child but with the purchase of a new house in a different community, a change of employment, or the visitation of illness or death. Homes, like persons, are changed by everything that happens to them. Persons who individually and as husband and wife can maintain command of life amid its many fluctuations and surprises are basically adequate.

Furniture and fixtures, finances and fortunes will change. Health and hopes will fluctuate, but the adequate marriage team will keep learning to be content in whatever state they must live. Changing family situations will dictate that they find happiness in a continually changing pattern, but happiness is there to be found if they will persistently discipline their own souls to meet it. The adjustment to change must be accomplished without diminshing the romantic adventure of persons who are deeply in love.

People who would make the most of marriage and home must learn to keep interested. There is plenty of excitement and challenge if they don't become too dull to see it. The great artist must be able to see beauty in the storm-boiled sea as well as in the sunset on a peaceful shore. The great poet must learn to feel and entertain great thoughts amid the pulsing of life's dark hours as well as in the soaring, ecstatic moments of romance at play. The couple who will make a good home must be able to keep their house furnished and their lives clothed with loveliness amid the constant kaleidoscopic change of life's ordinary contingencies.

A seasoned city editor, interviewing a young lady applicant for a reportorial job, asked her how she would go about writing a story about lovers. She said she would place it in a setting of a lily pond in the moonlight and lovers speaking tender words. He interrupted her to say that she knew little about life. "Love," he said, "is a person getting up at two o'clock on a cold morning to fix a hot-water bottle for someone and not feeling sorry for himself for having to do it." Love is living with the everydayness of things without losing life's essential sense of adventure.

Marriage responsibilities must be fulfilled amid escalating assignments. Each year of the existence of a marriage demands more from the persons involved. If they are making adequate growth they feel no strain in meeting these enlarged demands. They who would be continually sufficient for life must know every night that they are insufficient for the next day, and every year that the next one will tax them beyond their present qualifications. They must be prepared to grow in stature and find their greatest reward in personal becoming rather than in material achievement. Effective living is like rowing up a swift stream. One must row vigorously to keep even and only the energetic will go upstream. People who quit demanding more of themselves will soon be inadequate marriage partners.

Great men spend most of their time doing the same things as are done by mediocre men. They must live by the same general routine of eating, sleeping, bathing, and shaving. They must go to and from work, take time out for social life, and make room for other people to invade their busy world. They are known as great men because they do a few things more excellently than others can do them. Their ability to excel in these few assignments, however, is possible because in all of their living they discipline themselves more sternly. They perform greater assignments because they have become more capable persons.

Homes which are outstandingly rewarding are, likewise, much like the mediocre homes which surround them. They must deal with the same essential routines but they have disciplined themselves to make better use of the experiences they have at hand. The finest homes on earth are made amid the clutter of "dailyness" which environs all people.

The disciplines which make for adequacy in marriage and homelife are actually nothing more than the ability to keep command of commonplace things. No home will collapse under crises if it is continually well-disciplined in relation to the daily demands of mature responsibility.

It is neither possible nor necessary that people have a complete list of the hazards surrounding a marriage nor a prescription for all the cures. Each marriage must arrive at an emotional and spiritual stature which enables it to find a way to cope with life's contingencies. If people are sufficiently mature and sincere, they will recognize any erosive factor and deal with it promptly and prudently. In order, however, to provide a basis for recognizing such dangers a few of the most subtle perils are listed below. These are not the only predatory problems with which marriages are attacked nor are they essentially the most serious. They are simply a few of the many things which appear quite harmless until they establish their intrusion. Once they are accepted as part of a marriage pattern they proceed to erode all that is lovely.

When Habits Inhabit Homes. Never take a bear cub for a pet. It will become a big bear if it is kept and fed. Without a doubt the cub is cute, playful, and quite harmless but it will outgrow its controls. Habits are like bear cubs in a marriage. Most homes which are made intolerable are the victims of habits which were allowed to form before their ugly nature was recognized. A thoughtless mate does or leaves undone things which are not of themselves worth making a fuss about. Because the spouse and children love the person, they say nothing and pass the matter off lightly. However, since the guilty member of the family got by with the delinquency, it may easily be repeated until it becomes a habit. The cub has become a bear and has already invaded the rights of other members of the family. Bad habits never stay insignificant, even though they may not be basically immoral or dangerous. When they erode, even slowly, the cooperative adventure of the marriage, they are deadly. When any person becomes habituated to getting by with selfishness, that person becomes decreasingly desirable as a family member.

Speaking unkindly to one another is a habit which starts subtly but grows into a desperate monster. At first a tired person allows a bit of harshness or an irritating tone to color the voice ever so slightly. As this is repeated even a few times it seems more acceptable and the harshness invades more and more deeply into the conversation. The person habituated to speaking in this way eventually feels no inner compunction about it. However the people who listen to it never become sufficiently habituated to it to accept it. They may become calloused enough to pay no attention, so that the irritating voice must be raised higher and higher in order to get results, but they resent the voice more and more. Few habits will erode marriage and home situation so rapidly as will that of nagging, complaining, fretting, and screaming.

Such a habit starts in one member of the household and like an infection it spreads slowly to all of the family until every member of the family is quarreling and fussing. Eventually it makes the house such an unpleasant place that each member of the group seeks to spend as much time away from it as possible.

Prudent couples will help each other avoid falling into such a habit. It is easy for a person to form an erosive habit without being fully aware of it and sometimes loved ones should tell them frankly of its existence. Little cubs not only make big bears but they multiply until there is a house full of them. Many places where happy homes used to exist are now only dens where snarling bears claw at each other day and night.

Some dangerous habits have their beginnings in playful but unwise practices. People should never do in fun something they cannot live with if it becomes a habit. It may be very funny for a wife to get her husband in a public spot and tell some embarrassing joke on him. A husband, likewise, can get a big laugh out of making his wife the butt of a joke as he entertains the crowd. The things told on each other are not necessarily immoral nor demanding of secrecy. The difficulty is that someone is embarrassed and he doesn't enjoy it. In order to keep even, the injured person will wait an opportunity to return the joke in kind, and soon a habit is formed by which a husband and wife are always jabbing at each other before their friends. The result is that shortly social life becomes less desirable for one or both. More and more social invitations are either not gotten or are rejected and the two people are fenced in more and more with themselves. In this confined situation their jabbing remarks become even more personal until there is no peace. Cutting words are spoken with greater frequency. Voices habitually fall into tones of irritation and the home is well on the way to being destroyed entirely. What a shame that two people who loved each other so much as to get married should destroy their home by such an unnecessary and miserable habit!

There is no family which can always have the house well kept. There will be times when they will have to leave hastily with the sink full of dirty dishes, the beds unmade, and the furniture in disarray. No home will suffer badly from occasional situations of this sort, but if they become habitual they amount to a way of life. They eventually create a pattern of shabby living, reflecting undisciplined personalities and anti-social people. This kind of habit forms readily and soon spreads to the whole area of living. People become careless about their preparation for life's assignments. They often become habitually late in arrival at appointments. They become less interested in their homes, so that they spend less evenings together there. They are less proud of their home, so that they invite friends in less often. They are so far behind with their work that to invite friends in requires more housecleaning in preparation than they want to tackle. So they pass up the opportunity to share their hospitality. The children cease to bring their friends in, spending more time with their friends in other homes or elsewhere. The wife finds herself going to the neighbors for coffee rather than having them come in for a break. It all started with a habit which would never have been formed if they had known how it would grow.

This kind of housekeeping is much harder work than good housekeeping and yet the housewife gets no credit for the work she does. She never seems to get caught up. She is called lazy, shiftless, and a poor housekeeper when actually she may work harder than the good housekeeper who lives next door. She is struggling along, chained by a bad habit. This habit, once formed, will change the total temperament of a home and family.

Habits are as much a part of mealtime as are knives, forks, and spoons. They are as much a part of the meal as are the dishes of food. Go into a number of homes at an ordinary mealtime and you will find they all have basically similar food, similar table service, and similar appetites. But there the similarity ends. In one home the food is eaten with order and the other in chaos. In one home there is laughter and in the other there is jangling. In one home there are good manners while in the other there is boorishness. The difference is in the habits formed by a family. Usually the family with bad habits must spend much more for food than the one with good habits. Bad mealtime habits make for finicky appetites, wasted food, and irritated allergies. Few things contribute more to bad health, nervous troubles, ulcers, and tensions than bad habits formed by a family around their mealtime exposure to one another.

Mealtime is an easy place for habits to take root and grow because it provides more situations of exposure to the other members of the family. It is a time when each should respect the other, when each should conform to the family rules, and when no individual is entirely alone. If a mother is ever inclined to scold, she will find an occasion for it most often at mealtime. If a dad is inclined to be cross, grumpy, and unkind, he will be irritated into expression of it more often at mealtime. Mealtime is an ideal time for things to be spilled, broken, or upset. It provides an opportunity for selfishness to show itself most readily. It provides a time when conversation can become loud and competitive if it is unchecked. If anything has gone wrong all day, it will likely come to the fore in the mealtime situation.

There must certainly be some discipline, some order, and someone in command of the mealtime meeting of the family. If any member of the family allows an irritating habit to form and grow around the mealtime gathering, it will communicate very quickly to the other members of the family, who will feel they must outscream, out-scold, and out-irritate at every opportunity. What a pity that good food should be consumed by snarling, growling, quarreling, slapping bears just because a husband or wife brought a cub home and kept it! No family should allow such a habit to take root in the homelife. If it is tolerated a very few times, it will soon grow too big to handle. Form good habits and watch them with care. Mealtime habits are the most honest expression of what a home is actually like at heart.

Clothes Expose a Person. People never look far enough to see the heart of a tramp. They just look at his clothes and pass him by. The kind of clothes you wear and the way you wear them show the whole world what you are like. Clothes not only cover you; they expose you—not only the clothes you wear personally but the way you clothe your house, your table, and your yard. People form first impressions of you the minute they see your clothes. Most people will not go downtown or to church without making themselves quite presentable. They put on becoming garments for street wear, church wear, or play wear. That is fine, for people will think well of a becomingly dressed person.

Since we all like to be admired, we know we should be dressed in such a manner as to be socially accepted. Not only does it make a difference in how you look to others but it makes a big difference in the way you feel. You feel very differently when appropriately dressed than when you are not.

In the home we do not dress in our finest clothes. Dinner gowns would be inappropriate for wear while scrubbing floors, and delicate fabrics are impractical for a woman doing the laundry. Yet there is a sense in which many people rob themselves by careless dress at home.

It is more important that you make a good impression at home than at any other place on earth. If the people downtown think you dress too carelessly, you may lose their good opinion and become the subject of their coffee time gossip, but you can still go home and live in peace. However, if your appearance embarrasses your family, you have lost something you cannot get along without. It is much more important that a woman's husband think she is attractive than that the banker be impressed. It is much more important that a man's wife think he is handsome than that the waitress in the restaurant or the manager of the store be so impressed.

Many people think that the minute they are inside the walls of home their clothes cease to make any difference. This is where they are wrong. Clothes make more difference in the home than outside, for the good impression made at home is the most important one on earth.

No woman should dress extravagantly while doing housework nor try to appear like a millionaire matron while mothering a group of hungry children. Yet every woman must keep her own self-respect and the respect of her family by being neat, well-groomed, well-combed, and attractive. The most important person to come to the door all day is the man who comes home to that door at night. He should be met by a woman whose looks, appearance, and attire make him proud and glad to be home. Nothing can so frustrate a man as to be met night after night by a woman who looks like a hag, is dressed like a scarecrow, and speaks like the whining of an ailing pup.

It costs no more to be neat than to be untidy. It is a matter of habit and attention. It costs nothing to comb the hair, to wash a dress, or to freshen up a face.

Men, possibly more than women, are prone to become careless about their appearance when they are at home. Many times they complain that their wives are not as interested in them as they should be, are less affectionate than they used to be, and spend too little time talking with them. Maybe if they stopped to think how they allow themselves to look around home they would understand. No woman should have to live with a man who reeks of sweat and body odors. Of course he will have to work and will come home sometimes sweaty, but a man's hide is made of washable stuff. All it takes is a little pride, soap, and water. He can then be clean, well-shaved, and well-combed. No man should come to the table half dressed nor slouch around the house so unkept as to be afraid neighbors might come in and find him unpresentable. A husband should be constantly on the alert to make himself attractive to the most important woman on earth. It costs nothing but a little time and effort to be a man of whom a woman is proud and with whom she likes to associate.

Husbands and wives are ordinarily careful of their appearance when they go out, so that their mates will be proud of them and proud to go with them. They should be no less careful about the house. They should so attire themselves and groom themselves that even at night they are as beautiful and attractive as they can be. The person who insists on dressing like a tramp will soon be treated quite as one.

The way the house is kept, the way the children are kept, and the way people keep themselves become the expression of the home. The clothes may cover the skin but they undress the real person. People looking at the surface form an opinion of the person within.

Clean children behave better than children constantly dirty. A well-groomed man stands straighter, speaks more prudently, and becomes more dependable than an unkempt one. The wife and mother who is neat, crisp, and clean finds it easier to live a well-ordered day, perform well-planned work, and be an adequate mother. The opinion you form of yourself is important. It is quite an accurate measure of the real person.

Houses Are Made to Live in

Of course we want nice houses and nice furnishings. We would be less than normal if we did not, yet these things can become our masters. Sometimes people become so concerned about the house that they forget the folks who live in it. A man who is so concerned about protecting his fine house that he lays impossible or unreasonable demands upon his family will make the family wish they had never seen the new house. It is better to live in an old house where you can really live and laugh, work and play, than to live in a castle where you mustn't touch anything. Good housekeeping is a must. It is not fair to allow children to grow up in a home without learning to take care of it. They must learn to keep things in place, keep things clean, and keep them undamaged, but they need to live there with the idea that the house is a place for living rather than just for showing. When a wife and mother is more concerned about the compliments of guests than about the children who live there, she should get a job as curator in a museum.

On the other hand, it is unfair to allow children to run through the house so that when they go to the homes of your friends they are unwanted. Children need to be trained so well that neighbors and relatives will be sincerely glad to see them coming. If they are not, the child is put in a position of having to live in a world where people are all against him. If people don't like to have him come, he knows it. If he is unwanted, he knows it. The result is a badly damaged person. Children must learn to live congenially in a well-kept house so that their lives outside the home may benefit from it. The house should belong to the child as much as to the parents, but the parent must help the child learn to use it.

Even a husband should be made to feel at home in a house. Some husbands are definitely outsiders of the worst order in their own houses. They mustn't sit here, step there, or walk yonder. They mustn't sit where an ornamental pillow has first place nor lounge and read where the best, most comfortable chair is placed. If a wife is more concerned about showing off the furniture than in making her husband comfortable and happy she is missing the point. Of course houses should be well-kept, they should be furnished proportionate to the financial ability of the family, and every member of the family from Dad to the youngest child must take a responsibility in keeping them up. But they should still be places to live in rather than prisons.

When Big Feet Get in the Way. Did you ever find yourself sitting in a narrow passage where your feet were constantly in the way? It is a most miserable feeling. You've no place else to go, there's no way to turn around, and yet there just isn't room for your feet. Nobody is blaming you, nobody scolds you, but you know you're in the way. Oh, those big feet!

Sometimes when two people go about making a home they don't make room enough for each other's feet and they're constantly stumbling over each other. He tries to get over and meddle in her housekeeping, and the first thing he knows, he's on her toes. She tries to tell him how to run his business affairs and then projects, and soon she is on his toes. There isn't room enough in their little empire for both of them. The result is that both of them, trying to fill both places, are getting pretty sore toes.

To keep well-shaped, healthy toes, it is better for the home to have a place where each can have foot room. A man sitting around the house is the most bothersome thing a woman can put up with. His huge feet are under her, tripping and hindering her every time she turns around. No woman can do her work well with a man underfoot. However, the opposite is true too. No man can do his work well if every time he turns around his wife is complaining that he is on her toes. Office chairs are not made for two. Most men do better work if they are trusted by their wives to be men of decision and prudence. Of course they must both talk things over with the other, but they must each have an empire where they are undisputedly making the decisions.

There will be many times when the wife will need help. She will have a right to expect it, and no worthy husband will be unwilling to help. However, he should keep in mind that he is helping her, not running the house, and should not start some big reform just because he was asked to help rearrange the room or to paint the ceiling.

Some women marry men who are better cooks than they, but if the man is as good at being a husband as he is at cooking he will forget how to cook and forget it fast. Why should he humiliate his wife by knowing more about her domain than she knows or by having her come and ask him to make the gravy?

Sometimes a woman knows more about bookkeeping than her husband but she must use care and give a lot of thought before she takes on the job of keeping the family checkbook in balance. Don't take this over if it might make him overconscious of his lack of knowledge at this point.

Jump out of the Frying Pan. A house may be quite small and yet meet the need of a sizeable family if there is a big yard around it. People need room and that room cannot all be enclosed by the walls of a house. Happy families have room for living in areas surrounding the house.

Families need recreation, camping, outdoor cookouts, backyard barbecues, and many experiences which enable them to jump out of the close confinement of being housed up together. They should have as many overflow experiences as is possible. The family which is too contained inside its walls becomes tense, intense, and irritable.

People need neighbor families with whom they visit back and forth and with whom they can enjoy activities, both inside the house and out of doors. Widening the social experience to include friends of another family tends to decrease some of the pressures which build up when folks are too proximately exposed within their own family.

The school is a very wholesome overflow area for the children, providing them with many fine experiences which widen their world. The school does not become a substitute for the home but a supplement to it. It does not become the center of the child's life, for the home must remain central. The school must be an auxiliary area into which the child can go as into a big yard, thus broadening his life and at the same time taking pressure off the home.

The Church Is the Finest, Biggest Yard a Home Can Have. No other institution in the community can provide the fine social, cultural, religious, and educational experience which is found in the church. The church provides for the entire family. The school provides an area of experience and overflow only for the children. The job provides outside experiences and acquaintances for the father. To a more limited degree community activities provide stimulating outlets for the wife and mother. But each of these is limited to only part of the family. The church exposes the entire family to the same experiences and makes them acquainted with the same people. It provides an occasion for them to dress up at the same time, get into the car together, and go someplace together.

Not only does the church expose the family to a social experience which includes them all but it relates them as a family to God. The act of worship together dignifies the family. The adult participation in the act of worship makes religion an adult thing toward which children eagerly reach as they strive for adult status. No family is really complete until and unless God is a recognized Member of it. Learning of God broadens life, and broadened lives make adequate family members. Going to church is unmeasurably more than a social experience. To worship together, to include God, to know and love God as members of a family, gives a dimension to the home which could not be attained otherwise.

When God Moves in, Everybody Has More Room. When another person moves in, we all have to pull in our elbows to make room at the table and pull in our feet to make room on the floor; but when God moves in, people become less selfish, they require less room for themselves, they do less bickering and more loving. They do more giving and less asking, more serving and less bossing. Two people, selfish and without God, can be more crowded in a large house than a large family in a small house where the love of God is prevalent. A rancher one time was faced with a shortage of shed room for his herd of cattle. The herd had increased but his shed had not. He noticed that the long-horned cattle were taking up more room than they needed to take, so he dehorned them and found that the shed was plenty large for the entire herd. Horns take up a lot of room. When a family have horns and are continually digging each other's ribs, it is quite impossible to house them in the same building, be it ever so large. Take off the horns and you won't have to build a bigger house so soon. God in the lives of people helps them learn to love each other.

FINE ARTS, FINE FEATHERS, AND FINE BIRDS

Fine feathers do not make a fine bird, neither do fine trimmings make a fine house, but the fine arts are valuable in homemaking. The colorings, the arrangements, the decor, and the order of the house cannot but affect the members of the household. Every woman should study decorating either formally or informally, so that she can make the best possible use of the things she can afford. Some women without training lack the artistic sense to make a home look lovely, even with the finest furnishings and a free checkbook. Others can take a minimum of money, a few secondhand pieces of furniture, some odds and ends of wedding presents, and some remnants of material and make an old house look like a palace. There is a knack to placing furniture, hanging pictures, draping drapes, and arranging flowers. It is not the cost of an article so much as the placement of it that makes it contribute to the loveliness of a room.

Every home should be made as beautiful as it can be made. Sometimes it can be done with inexpensive annual flowers. Sometimes a little wintertime planning, springtime planting, and summer gardening can keep flowers in the home all summer and fall. Sometimes wives make a hobby of going to junk shops and picking up furniture which has neither value nor apparent potential but with sandpaper, varnish, and vigor they make it into something worthy of a very fine home.

Good music should have a place in every household. There is a difference between mere racket to fill a house with noise, and good music to fill the atmosphere with inspiration and uplift. In these days almost any family can afford some kind of record player and a few good albums. The finest music in the world is available at little cost to those who will pick it well. Children and adults will be alike inspired and calmed by music which has real meaning and quality.

The dinner table does not need extravagant food but it does need decor which is in good taste. A simple meal, attractively served, will do people more good than an extravagant one thrown on without thought to aesthetic values. It takes more than food to make a good meal. It takes beauty and loveliness and happiness. Every family needs a daily table well set and an occasional "banquet" experience in their own dining room. Children should learn to eat at well-set tables. The people whose meals are thrown on the table—bread in the loaf, milk in the bottle, and jam in the jar—will be physically well-fed when they wolf it down but they will lack something essential in the real values of the meal. Mealtime should be a time of inspiration, uplift, and spiritual refreshment as well as a time for stuffing food in mouths.

A few extra dishes can be washed without much more work. A couple of candles are not very expensive. A tablecloth can be done up occasionally for the sake of giving the family a little more sense of culture at mealtime. An extra knife, fork, and spoon at each place can be afforded occasionally so that the family does not forget how to eat comfortably in a more formal situation.

Grace at Meals Is for Big People. Every home should have the dignity, the reverence, and the natural gratitude to pause and thank God for the blessings they are enjoying. Some families make mealtime merely a time when the food comes up for grabs the minute they reach the table. They never wait for each other and have about the same table manners as hungry animals. They do get some food all right but they starve their souls.

Any family has time enough to wait until all are seated, then have some form of ritual of thanks. Some families have a memorized table grace which the entire family quotes in unison. This is good in that it gives a chance for all members to participate. This is particularly desirable when the family makes no pretense at being deeply religious and none feel qualified for offering a prayer. This type of table ritual is used in many very devout homes and it is good. Some families have a table grace which they sing in unison and this has, likewise, a very fine value.

It is more common for one member of the family to pray a short, extemporaneous prayer of thanksgiving while all members of the family sit with bowed heads. This is very often under the direction of either the mother or father, preferably the father, who either offers the short prayer himself or calls upon some other member of the family or an occasional guest for the prayer. The children are eager to participate as early in life as possible, and under the example of their parents they soon learn to say short and very interesting prayers. They often enjoy this practice so much that the parents call upon them quite frequently. Thus, at almost every meal a child does the praying. This is fine in that it gives the child a sense of participation, but it is bad in that it makes the whole experience into a childish activity. It ceases to be an adult project in which the child is honored to participate but a children's experience which the parents have outgrown. With this attitude it will not be long until the children will feel it is outgrown by them and is to be dropped.

Some rules should be followed in all the religious activities of the home. Whether it be in the table grace or in the family prayer time, prayers must be kept short and meaningful. Participation should be directed by the parent, and it should be kept before the family as an adult activity in which the children are honored to

70

participate and an activity which they should lead when they become heads of their own homes. These devotional experiences should always be kept in a setting of kindness, happiness, and relaxed goodwill. They should be kept so interesting that the children will never want to miss them.

Dollars and Darlings. A couple or a family can be happy without many cents, provided they have plenty of sense. However, the minute they try keeping up with the Joneses, or try to buy happiness by purchasing more things, they are in for trouble. Much of our spending is the result of our boredom and many families could live more cheaply if they were happier. When people become bored with their lives they try to drown their boredom with things. Things cost money and they never satisfy. A woman who becomes bored with her home and housekeeping can break even a rich husband with her spending. She thinks she is really economizing, too, for she spends so much less than she wants to spend. It does not take much money for a contented person to live on. Smart husbands should know that the happier they keep wives the cheaper they are to support. Wives should learn that about husbands, too. It takes a lot of money to support a person who is bored. The person who has limited financial means should of all people learn to enjoy life and to be interested in the daily things which environ his or her spot on the earth.

The Wedding Dress and the Marriage Dress. A woman has only one wedding dress and it may be made of satin and lace, pearls and brocade. It is a work of art and fills a real need for her in a very important hour of life. She never wears it out and never needs to replace it. Her marriage dress can be simple gingham, print, percale, or jersey. It may even be denim or twill, but it is practical. It wears out and must be replaced time after time. She has several of these dresses, so

71

that she can often change; but a marriage dress is made for working in, for going to church, to town, or to visit the neighbors. A marriage dress is worn to the door when her husband comes in at night and to the table when she serves her family. There is a lot more demand made on the marriage dress than on the wedding dress. Marriage dresses have to be washable, cleanable, alterable, and comfortable. The man, likewise, has a wedding suit and a marriage suit, the latter to wear every day as he comes to grips with commonplace toils and tasks.

A home is more than a marriage fitted into a house. It is everything about a marriage related to everything about a house and poured into the total lives of the people involved. A home is a house alive with people, crawling with activity, struggling with burdens, adjusting to situations. A home is people laughing and crying, working and playing, hoping and aspiring. A home is a whole human adventure distilled into the essence of naked, undiluted personality and subjected to both the dullness and the adventure of having to do with living persons.

Lo, children are a heritage from the Lord,
The fruit of the womb is a reward.
Like arrows in the hand of a warrior,
So are children of one's youth.
How happy is the man
Whose quiver is filled with them!
PSALMS 127:3-5*

CHAPTER FOUR

An Invasion by Babies

The world has had a lot of invasions which are written up in the history books. There have been the invasions by nomadic hordes. There have been invasions by armies and invasions by colonists. There have been invasions by philosophies, ideologies, and concepts. There have been bloody invasions and peaceful ones. But the most upsetting, the most invincible, telling, and exciting one is the invasion by babies.

The Bible: An American Translation, J. M. Powis Smith, Edgar J. Goodspeed. Copyright 1923, 1927, 1948 by the University of Chicago Press.

Imagine it! An invasion by a baby! A tiny baby, unable to walk or speak, unable to plan or to prosecute a plan, unable to carry weapons or to read maps, can effect an invasion into the most solidly occupied area of all mankind—the home. This invasion is destined not only to provide a place for the fulfillment of the invader but a situation for the fulfillment of every life inhabiting the area of occupation.

A Baby Takes up a Lot of Room. No person who has seen a baby come home from the hospital will deny the fact that it completely invades the house, possesses the household, and takes command of the resources. Houses which always seemed quite large and ample suddenly are too small, and rooms which were spacious when occupied by a man and woman become cluttered impossibly when a tiny six-pound bundle of infant moves in. It doesn't make sense that a person so small should so completely reorder the household or make such terrific demands upon adults, but it is so. The little person who rules from the bassinet begins to decide when the adults will wake or sleep, eat or work, wash or scrub, go to town or stay home, and a lot of other things. That baby decides how many evenings out the parents shall have and how much money they will be permitted to spend on themselves.

That monarch in the cradle, that tyrant in the tinsel, what a ruler with an iron hand! People who have never brought a baby home have a lot to discover, for nobody can tell them what to expect. They have to experience the take-over before they will believe it. Babies take up a lot of room and they take it by force in one great landing. Things around the house will never return to normal once a baby arrives. Life simply establishes new norms in an adjusted situation.

There is a great difference between an invasion of an unoccupied frontier and the enforced occupation of property already occupied by others. When the people from the Old Country began to invade North America, it was chiefly a problem of pushing the wilderness back. Apart from the displacement of a few Indians, there was little struggle save the inevitable conflict with the forest, prairie, and climate. However, when the armies under the allied command of General Eisenhower invaded Europe, landing on the Normandy beachhead, it was a very different situation. This was not simple, for other people were already there and in possession. There were farmers and villagers who owned every foot of ground. There were people living there; there was also the most powerful army ever massed on European soil. The struggle was to the death. If babies came in to occupy a wilderness, an area not already occupied, it would be more simple; but when a baby comes, it is essentially true that he or she comes to a home which is already full of people.

A husband and wife fill a home full of themselves. They have established a partnership which includes the whole area of their occupation. Their lives belong to each other. Their rooms, their time, their affections, and their attentions are mutually shared in the partnership of marriage. When a baby comes into this situation, some adjustment is essential. It means that both members of the partnership will have less of themselves to give to their mate, for they must give something of themselves to the baby. They will have less time, less attention, and less money. They will both be involved so that their complete absorption with one another is forever gone. They must not only be content to receive a bit less of their mate but they must face the fact that they are giving less of themselves to their mates and must compensate in some manner if their partnership obligations are to be preserved.

An Invasion by a Baby Is Not a Temporary Thing. As long as the parents live, the area taken over by the baby will continue to be claimed. The area of possession will increase rather than diminish. From the moment a couple is aware that a baby is on its way, they are never to be free again from involvement with that new person coming into their lives. Every relationship will be altered by that involvement. Even if death should take the child at birth, in infancy or childhood, their lives are still involved.

If the child lives and matures, the parent will be involved even after the child marries and goes to a home of his or her own. The parent will still feel all the concerns and bear all the burdens throughout his or her remaining years. He will know all the warm surgings of love, the cold fog of fears, and the anxieties of the unknown for that offspring even though the new generation is more competent than the parent. No person gets over the invasion made by a baby.

The Partnership Area into Which the Baby Makes the Invasion Is Changed. Any partnership presents numerous problems of human adjustment, even though it be a very simple one. Business partnerships, whether they be an unwritten borrowing and loaning of the lawn mower or the management of a great corporation, will demand times of definition and reappraisal as well as of give-and-take.

Marriage is a partnership and as such involves the rights of two persons in a situation which will need constant updating, adjustment, and correction. The differences which arise in a partnership are not necessarily bad. In fact, the partnership which is completely agreeable is likely to be subject to atrophy and sterility. Usually the corporations or partnerships which are most successful are those which have the benefit of restless leadership and face constant change and correction. No marriage needs to be a partnership between people who always see eye to eye. It does not need to be a situation so agreeable as to allow its members to doze through their years. It needs rather to be an effective combination of personalities which stimulates and inspires, encourages and demands, climbs and calls the mate to climb. It is necessary, however, that an effective marital relationship be one where there is give-and-take on the part of both partners and where both put their total assets into the corporate investment.

No one can define or codify the specific plan by which two people can live together. Their success depends upon more than a plan. It includes a growing understanding, a mutual self-giving, and an eager sharing. The wholesomeness of a marriage is tested and should be also enriched by its response to the various traumatic experiences which come to it. These experiences come in the whole spectrum of living, including economic, social, religious, health, and career situations. No one can predict from which quarter the storm may break or in which area of life the crisis will appear, but every home must live through a continuing series of crises. These times when their strength is put to the test do not injure a wholesome marriage, but for the couple who lack the adequacy essential to effective living there is a certain impending collapse.

Few experiences in the home demand such wide adjustments as the arrival of a baby. If either of the adults in a home cannot adjust to make room for the baby, there is going to be trouble, not only between parent and child, but between parent and parent. When both members of the home are ready for the parental adventure, the necessary changes come happily and wholesomely; but, if not, they are painful.

What a Baby Does to a Home

No two homes are affected in the same manner and measure by the arrival of a child. Much depends upon the emotional, physical, and social readiness of the parents. If the child is wanted eagerly by both, it will obviously be a different set of circumstances to face than if it is unwanted by either or both. If the parents have been married only a year, the situation may be different from what it would be if they have been married twenty years. It is particularly acute if the parents are not yet wed. Sometimes the arrival of a child interrupts a career, stops an education, prevents some long-planned project, or in other ways interferes with the intended routine of the household.

In cases where a child arrives unwanted, the frustration caused is often inflicted unwittingly upon the innocent baby. Even though the baby might not be consciously blamed for the interruption of a planned routine, the parents often go through the experience with a wrong attitude. It becomes an ordeal rather than the adventure it should have been. Parents should adjust their own attitudes sufficiently to give the baby and themselves the fullest possible opportunity for fulfillment. It is quite impossible for unwilling parents to be entirely good parents. If people are going to be parents, they should adjust their pattern of life and their plans so that they can be wholesome, eager persons for the sake of all concerned.

The most difficult adjustment to parenthood is that which must be made by unwed parents. We wish that this were not so frequent a situation and that when it happens it would always happen on the other side of town. But in our so-called sophisticated society the problem of unwed parents is increasing alarmingly.

As was stated in a previous chapter, in many cases marriage of the involved couple is the best way to deal with their dilemma—the dilemma of involved relatives and even the problems of the unborn child. If a reasonable chance for successful marriage exists, the couple should marry quickly. However, in case the couple does not have a reasonably good chance for success in marriage, it is foolish to involve their lives more deeply than they are already involved. To marry merely to give a name to the child when the home to which the child is born will be unhappy or inadequate is unkind to all concerned. It simply means that the hardships involved are postponed by the adults until the child will have to bear them too. If the child is born into a temporary marriage, it will certainly be forced to spend its most formative months in a marriage situation which is bitter, frustrating, and unhappy.

Sometimes the mother-to-be insists on going ahead and bearing her child in loneliness and caring for it as a mother would. This is the very normal yearning of the woman but it is unfair to the child who will be forced into the situation of being always marked as an illegitimate child. Though the mother may have some story which she tells the child to cover up the ugly facts, in due time the truth will come out and the child will suffer for it. Sometimes the parents of the unfortunate girl insist on taking the baby and rearing it as their own. They can truly give it all the love and care a child could have, but they cannot give it legitimacy. This is impossible in such a situation.

If by the imprudence of unwed people a child is called upon to invade an ugly adult situation, there is no way to give legitimacy to the birth other than for the couple to marry or for the child to be placed for adoption. If the marriage does not have a good chance for success, the adoption plans are far better. These adoptions should be handled by a legitimate, state-recognized agency or with dependable legal counsel. The mother-to-be or her parents, if she is a minor, should commit themselves in writing to this plan before the baby is born, so that there will be no question left to decide at the time. The mother or her parents should not see the baby or become attached to it, and the adoption should be by persons in another community sufficiently removed that there will be no likelihood of the true mother ever learning of the child's where-abouts or name. Thus the child is adopted into a home which will welcome it, will make it legitimate, and give it a life with no embarrassment.

In due time the mother, with no divorce in her past, may rise above her humiliation and have ample chance to love, to marry, and to bear children who can walk proudly at her side. There is no way whereby the unwed father can be made to bear his full share of the burden, but he should be morally obligated to financial responsibility for the expenses involved.

The first obligation of the unwed parents is to care for the interests of the person who is arriving as a baby. The entire lifetime of the person is ahead and should not be blemished or complicated by the undisciplined living of the persons who are responsible for his or her arrival.

When it is prudent for the couple to marry and make a home for themselves and their soon-coming child, they should never try to avoid embarrassment by altering the dates on their marriage certificate or on the baby's birth certificate. These are legal documents, and to tamper with them or ask officiating persons to adjust them is perjury. Serious legal problems can result, even many years down the line.

Often adults who find themselves unexpectedly committed to new parenthood are deeply frustrated. Sometimes they are young adults with plans for completing college or getting out of debt. Sometimes they are couples with small babies already in the home, and sometimes they are people who just don't want babies. Whatever the reasons for their indisposition to it, they are going to have the baby. They have by their own acts already fixed the decision that the baby will come, and they may as well start preparing for the invasion. The emotional preparation is often more difficult than the physical. The inclination to blame each other for the accident is folly. It is true that either of them may have been selfish, thoughtless, or careless but both must make up their minds that they are going to have a baby in the house and begin to adjust to the idea. All the ugly words, resentments, and accusations in the world cannot change the fact which they have created for themselves, and mature adults will give up whatever other adventures they had planned and set out to pursue this experience to its fullest enjoyment. In the years to come they are usually most thankful for the baby. They must by all means make their adjustment before the baby arrives and never require the baby to fight for a place in an unwelcome climate.

Babies and Rocking Chairs. It is a painful surprise to an older married couple who have reared their family, and think their childbearing years have passed, to have the doctor diagnose her irregular health as being due to pregnancy. Often embarrassment, chagrin, and fear take hold of them. They had made plans for the years when their children were grown and now they must start the whole process over again. They sense that by the time this baby is through college they will be too old for the plans which they had made. Their whole life pattern must be rearranged.

Such couples should forget their embarrassment, for there is nothing embarrassing about parenthood in the framework of marriage and legitimacy. It is life's noblest adventure and should be accepted with humility and reverence. Almost invariably these late-in-life babies are the most enjoyed of all and bring the mature years finer compensations than are brought by their children who came earlier. It is true that the emotional, physical, and social adjustments are more difficult to make. However, here again the first duty is to the baby. These adults should remember that most of their lives are past and the child has an entire lifetime ahead, so everything possible should be slanted toward the effective rearing of the child.

Parents are often inclined to spoil the late-in-life baby. They become more attached to the child because of the fact that life has fewer involvements to compete for their interest. They have more financial security and can provide more liberally for this child. They are already feeling the loneliness occasioned by the absence of their grown family. Usually they are more easily upset and nervous than are younger couples and frequently are more inclined to let the child get away with undisciplined conduct. Furthermore, the gap between the generations is continually widened by the great change in our way of life, so that it is more difficult for the parent and child to have a meeting ground in contemporary thinking. Such parents must seek always to secure the good of the child ahead of their own enjoyment. It is their responsibility to prepare the child for a lifetime rather than to find personal entertainment or pleasure for their own later years. They must always remember that to spoil a baby is to spoil a person.

Babies by Adoption Make an Invasion Too. Couples who adopt babies usually do so because they desire a baby and cannot bear one as the physical fruit of their own marriage. Such people are usually mature, financially able to support the child, and emotionally ready, eagerly ready, for the arrival. To them the baby comes as a result of careful planning, long waiting, and deliberate business dealing. In most cases these babies find a very fine home and these parents have an enriching experience. Without a doubt the adoption of babies by such parents is advisable, rewarding, and in the best interest of both the adoptive parents and the adopted baby. It is true that the parents have missed the nine months of emotional preparation which God ordained that they should have, but they have experienced many compensating things.

Apart from the method and techniques of arrival, the adopted baby should not be in the least different from the baby born of the parents who will make it a home. No attempt should be made to hide from the child the fact that he is adopted. It should be an accepted fact long before he understands all the implications. He should be assured of the fact that the parents wanted him so much that they took this step. If the fact of the child's being adopted could be forever kept secret, there might be some arguments in favor of not telling him he was born to parents other than the ones he has learned to love as Mother and Father. However, life does not keep our secrets well and down the line someplace, maybe after the child has reached adult years, he will discover in checking a legal paper or by some other means that he was adopted. Under no circumstances must the child receive the information from a secondary source such as the neighbor's children. It is so much better if it be learned and shared in the confidential, warm setting of the family rather than coming as a shock from some unexpected and unkind source.

To all intents and purposes adopted children should be treated exactly the same as children born into the home. They should be loved, disciplined, and provided for in equal measure. No effort should be made to look up their natural parents. No derogatory things should be said of them. Nothing should be done to give the child any feeling of insecurity because of the unknown or uncertain past.

Parents of adopted children should minimize the influence of heredity. Most children are less influenced by heredity than we think. Most of what is attributed to native influence is environmental influence, and if the adoptive parents have the child from infancy they must accept responsibility for most of the bents of the person. A baby is much more the product of the home in which he is reared than of the parents to which he was born. If the child is adopted after attaining an age of four or five years, this is not true, for in that length of time the personality is greatly influenced. By the time a child has reached this age it is difficult to separate between the hereditary and the environmental markings. Many personality traits are quite established by that time.

Some Babies Arrive as Stowaways in a Marriage. This type of invasion is often the most difficult of all for both the child and the parents. The child is the natural child of one parent and the stepchild of the other. This kind of entrance into a home creates a major problem for the marriage—for the child as well as for each parent personally.

One of the first areas of problem arises from the fact that, by its very nature, marriage needs a time for adjustment, for intimacy, and for mutual acquaintance which is best gotten in privacy. In a normal marriage this time is provided by nature's deliberation, but in a marriage where children are already present this is impossible. The natural inclinations of the newly made husband and wife must be adjusted to the fact that they are not alone in the house. They want opportunity to say things, to talk of things, and to live together in a romantic abandonment which is forbidden by the peering, curious eyes of boys and girls. Thus the adults cannot but feel the intrusion and will unwittingly convey to the child the sense of his being an intruder. Few situations can be so painful and so injurious to a child as to feel that his very presence in the home is a problem. He in turn will take the attitude that the stepparent is an intruder into his life and his family. This can be the beginning of a lasting ordeal of suffering and loneliness which may damage the marriage as well as the child or children.

When adults who have children are contemplating marriage or when an adult contemplates marriage to a person with children, there needs to be some very serious emotional and educational preparation. This is not a simple project but is on many occasions very rewarding. It should be possible for two adults to make such adjustment as is necessary to provide a warm nest for children who are already stabbed by loneliness. Many are very happy throughout their lives in such homes, and we would not discourage the marriage of persons who have lost a companion, yet have been permitted to keep the children born of that companionship. Such persons are by the very nature of things older than most marriage mates and should be sufficiently mature to enable this greater adjustment to be made. Marriage when children are involved is an experience for mature people, capable of major responsibility.

The adults who bring children with them into a marriage should plan their steps carefully, as the total future of their lives is involved. They should understand each other so as to work as a team in matters of discipline, allowances, expenditure of money, and conduct in the home. They must go into the marriage fully expecting that they will have limited privacy, and knowing that the presence of the children will limit every other privilege they have a right to enjoy. The child must not be blamed for it.

It is more difficult for adults to feel close to a child whom they meet first through marriage rather than through birth. There is no substitute for the conditioning experience of nine months of waiting, weighing, and wonder. The marrying parents must keep in mind that the child has already endured the ordeal of losing a parent. The child has loved a mother or father who has cuddled, cared for, and companioned with him.

In the most impressionable years of his life, another person has been endeared to him. That person has been removed either by the shock of death or perhaps by the bitterness of a divorce. These traumatic experiences leave a much deeper mark on the child than adults realize. They leave him frightened, insecure, and inclined to become withdrawn. Into this tight world of the child's personal emotions the stepparent comes as an invader. If such an invasion is ever to be completely accepted, it will be through the wholesome efforts of both the parent and the stepparent. This readjustment is usually much more difficult if the previous marriage was terminated by divorce than though it ended by the death of a parent. Death is cruel but it is not bitter. It takes a parent but it does not leave an infected sore such as a broken home does.

The adults in such a marriage must take the lead and include the child warmly. The child cannot take the initiative and make a place for himself. This is a demanding assignment, but if the people involved are not willing and adequate for it they should not enter into a marriage which will be less desirable for the children than for them. Some stepparents fill the parental shoes fully and happily, which proves it can be done, but it should not be attempted by people who are selfish or immature.

Today's Moral Concepts Are Often Unfair to Babies. We agree that the male-female relationship in life is productive of many interesting experiences and exposures. Husbands and wives enjoy each other in many ways other than in reproduction, but we must never lose sight of the dignity and glory with which God adorned parenthood. To become a mother or father is a noble fulfillment of life and of the divine plan. Modern society often treats conception as only an accident which unfortunately is associated with certain physical enjoyments, and the birth of babies is treated as a mixture of misfortune and sometimes even disgrace. What a corruption of the plan of God! In all of life we are partners with God, but in no other area does God come so close to us and allow us such an adventure at His side as when He permits us to share with Him in bringing eternal, immortal persons into being. In this adventure we are expressing our pure love in humanity's noblest creative experience.

We must not allow the dignity of childbearing to be dissipated by the earthly definitions given to our marital relationships. Bringing children into the world may at times be inconvenient but it is not a disgrace. It may demand work and sacrifice but it also rewards us with life's finest fulfillment. It may deprive us of some immediate pleasures but it gives us eventually life's greatest satisfactions.

There is a cheap social ideology which makes it almost dishonorable to bear babies. It treats sex life as an end in itself to be enjoyed without regard to marital relations, moral obligations, or human responsibility. This is in part due to the commercialization of sex as a means of selling merchandise, packing theaters, and getting crowds into nightclubs. To all such commercial attitudes, childbearing is an inconvenience to be avoided.

Much of the newsstand printed matter and backroom conversation of these days treats sex life as something which succeeds best without reproduction and creates an ideology which looks upon conception and childbearing as indicating stupidity or ignorance. It is no wonder that many young people enter into marriage without the proper concepts in this regard and establish homes in which babies are not welcome. When babies invade such homes they are due to have a hard time making for themselves a wholesome place.

Babies Deserve a Climate of Godliness. Children yearn for love, for security and warmth. They are eager to learn of God and His love for them. They want to include God in their thinking.

Parents who leave God out of their plans in the conception, birth, and rearing of a baby will do the person a gross injustice. The baby in the home deserves an early acquaintance with holy things and with Deity. The child should be taught to pray, to believe, to recognize, and to love God.

When adults try to get along in the home without the benefit of a vital faith, they are robbing themselves. The whole idea of marriage and of parenthood was of God and should be dignified and enriched by the welcomed presence of Deity in every facet of living. When a husband and wife side by side draw near to God and experience the uplift of the divine resource, they will discover that parenthood takes on a new and more wonderful meaning. Both the parents and the child need to think of wrongdoing as sin against God as well as against people. They need to recognize the deadliness of evil when it is embraced in life. Parents who have no respect for God will have difficulty in instilling in the child a correct moral and spiritual ideal. The Christian home is not only a better place into which children can come but it is a more delightful place in which two love-bound people can live together in hallowed excitement and pleasure.

BABIES AND ADULTS

1. *Babies Invade Every Area of Adult Privileges.*

Before babies come it is possible for adults to put things in place and have them stay there. They can clean furniture and find it staying clean for a considerable time, wash windows and see them without fingerprints for a long time, or clean floors without likelihood of things being spilled or scattered on them. Babies change this. Things get disarranged when there is a baby in the house. The babies must be taught to respect all of these adult rights and eventually learn to enjoy the orderliness of the home as much as do their parents, but that learning process is not sudden nor short. Parents must accept responsibility to teach the child how to live in the situation rather than blaming babies for their invasion. Parents who come to think of the child as a nuisance will be very poor parents at best.

The house must belong to the baby too. Though it must still be the empire of the adults, the child is a member of the family also. The child must be permitted to enjoy the house and its furnishings rather than living under such constant restraint as to feel unwelcome. This does not mean that the child is to be allowed the run of the place nor that the baby should get by with all kinds of plundering. It simply means that the child should be treated as a member of the family who needs a place and needs certain rights in the house. He must have a place for his toys, his noise, his activity, and his play. He must be included in family fellowship and laughter. He must have room to live and learn. The house must be the baby's home as well as the mother's showplace or the father's retreat.

2. *A Baby Invades Adult Areas of Interest.*

What parent has not sometimes been annoyed by the perpetual questions, interruptions, and curiosities of a child? When the adult is trying to concentrate on an important task, the child is busy trying to learn all about it. If a tool is laid down, the child picks it up to experiment with it. If there is a move made, the child asks why, how, when, which way, and why not? This is the normal questing of a child who wants to absorb from the parent all that the parent knows and is. It is as natural for a child to seek knowledge and information from the parent as it is for him to look to the parent for food. The child thinks the parent has all the answers, knows everything, can do anything, fix anything, and explain everything.

No parent can possibly live up to all that a child believes, but neither can any parent afford not to give his or her absolute best to the child. He must never let him down. The child must have free access to the personality resources of the parent as well as the material and intellectual resources. Life's finest returns come to the child from being exposed to the parent. The child yearns for that exposure and will intensify it with every opportunity. By this means he is able to reach for self-fulfillment. The child must be rewarded with a wholesome self-giving on the part of the parent. We cannot escape the constant drain a child would make upon our inner resources without depriving the child of something important.

If the parent is interested in anything, the child invades that area and is interested too. If the parent wants to work in the garden, that is what the child will want to do. No matter what the parent sets out to do, the child will be right behind or beside with questions and offers of helpfulness.

3. *Babies Invade the Adult Social Situation.*

When the baby comes, the adult social life must undergo a radical change. Nights out will be less frequent, social engagements will be curtailed, and invitations to certain places will begin to diminish. No couple should feel robbed by the presence of the baby. After all, the baby is the most interesting, entertaining, and appreciative company on earth. Yet the parents must not become social hermits. They must not allow their social life to be too badly fenced in.

Parents need some nights out. On many occasions they can and should take the baby or babies with them. However, there should be times when they get a competent person to care for the baby while they have an evening to themselves. Sometimes parents shut themselves in so completely with the baby that they become unable to give the child as interesting a homelife as it needs. Parents cannot be at their best if they become bored, weary, or fenced in.

When people come to the home the baby should be treated as a member of the family, as a person with rights, feelings, and dignity. The baby should not be shown off as a pet, played with as a toy, talked about as a piece of furniture, nor in any way singled out as anything other than a member of the family. No baby should be allowed to monopolize the place nor the occasion. Give the child place but not the whole place. Teach the child to respect the places of the adults too.

The Couple Must Put Limits on the Invasion by Babies. In this we do not mean essentially the limiting of the number of babies who will enter the home but the limiting of the occupation of the parents' lives. If the parents are to provide a good home for the children, they must have a happy marriage. If they are to keep a cozy nest in which children can experience a wholesome childhood, they must keep their own romantic life aglow.

Sometimes unthinking parents give so much of themselves and their home to the baby that they rob each other and themselves of an indispensable ingredient. Husbands and wives need some space which is their own. They need their room, their bed, and their privacy for living. This does not indicate that they should push their children aside nor that they should be selfish with themselves, but it will be better for the baby to have his own bed and bedroom. It is best that the child not get the habit of spending either the first or last part of the night sleeping with the parents. The child must be cuddled, romped with, and given a wholesome welcome in the whole house but no living pattern

91

should be formed which deprives the husband and wife of some private domain.

The baby will invade time, too, beyond what the parents have available. There is no limit to the demands a child will make on the time of a parent if the parent allows his clock to be raided. Parents need some time for themselves too. They will not be good parents unless they have bits of life in which to enjoy each other. They need time to keep acquainted, to share their emotions, their thoughts, and their affections without interruption.

A baby invades the hearts of parents, too, and will occupy a very large place in the affections. This is as it should be, but it is not good for the parents to become so involved in loving the baby that they have no time for endearment and affection between themselves. It is good for a wife to play with the baby, but she must do a little playing with her husband too. It is fine for a husband to cuddle the baby, but he should not quit cuddling his wife. If in the process of giving attention to the baby the romance is lost from the marriage, the child will lose everything that could have been previously given by the attentive parent. The child needs to learn to share with others, and the basic place to learn this unselfish way of life is by being taught that Mother and Dad have rights in the home. If the baby gets between the parents, everybody will lose what they all cherish most.

Once the Baby Lands an Invasion, It Is for Keeps. A baby comes to stay and continue his or her occupation. He will pursue that occupation into constantly expanding areas of homelife. The baby in the bassinet occupies a lot of room but the toddler will start going places. When a baby establishes a beachhead in the home, the next thing parents know a growing boy or girl is in the home, then a teen-ager, a young adult, and then—grandchildren!

Many parents who are quite adequate for living with a baby in the home are incapable of making a good home for teen-agers. They can make room for the bassinet but cannot make room for the complicated gear of an emerging adult. When a baby arrives, parents should start growing along with it, for they will have to become much bigger persons to keep up with the growing needs of the one who has invaded their little world.

Many times emotionally immature parents become jealous and insecure in the presence of their own growing offspring. Sometimes a mother is shocked when her daughter is praised, complimented, and discussed as a charming young lady. The mother sees in the daughter a picture of herself in years gone by. The girl is trim, beautiful, charming, and winsome and the mother sees in the mirror something which compares unfavorably. The unspoken, gnawing fear of displacement emerges here. The mother is likely to make a blind effort to secure herself and her position by keeping the image of the girl cut back. When her husband brags on the girl, she starts to enumerate her faults. When he remarks about how beautiful the girl is, the mother will retort that she went off this morning without making her bed. She will accuse her of being careless, unruly, lazy, or in some other way less noble than the father thinks. The mother loves the girl but she is not personally adequate for accepting her as another woman in the house who may be more charming than she. This is quite often a problem between fathers and sons also —however, not usually as vicious as that between mother and daughter. It is seldom a problem between mother and son or father and daughter. Most fathers can readily accept the adult emergence of their daughters and, likewise, most mothers find no strain when a son becomes a young man.

Parents Cannot Keep the Baby Small. Sometimes parents who are more adequate for parenthood of babies than of teen-agers or young adults will unintentionally try to impede the progress of the child in order to assure the continuance of their authority and domain. They continue to make all decisions for the child long after the child should have learned to make decisions for himself. Mothers tell their children how to dress, bathe, care for themselves, and handle their daily routine long after the child is capable of self-reliance. However, the mother enjoys caring for a baby, enjoys having the baby dependent, and fears release of these little details lest it undermine her hold. She even talks "baby talk" in an effort to extend baby attitudes over a span reaching into young adulthood. Parents should discover the pleasures of living with growing people and be ready to give that child every opportunity and assistance in personal emergence. The more dispensable the parent can become without lessening the disciplines of the child, the better. The parent cannot stay always with the child, and to perpetuate indispensability beyond its essential purpose is to endanger the well-being of all concerned.

Good parents let their children "help" them. They help mothers make cookies and help fathers cultivate gardens. Of course they are clumsy and make more mess than they should but that is the way they learn. They must be trusted. God has trusted us, too. He has given us tools of our own and permitted us to watch Him at work and to help Him. At no place is this project of partnership with God so delightful as in the creation of persons. God always lets a man and a woman help Him create immortal individuals. He does not dominate us nor do everything for us. He gives us not only privilege but responsibility and we must rise to our full stature to be worthy of such trust.

God surrounded our creative adventure with the fragrant flowers of marriage and the sweet essence of romance. He associated it with pleasant sensations, lovely surroundings, and intimate communication. He then came near and touched it all with His own fingerprints and breathed into it the breath of His likeness and called the product your child and mine. This is not just a baby. This is a person.

The ones who happen now to be babies are the persons who will eventually till our farms, manage our industries, or govern our states. That baby will eventually arrange our funeral and settle our estate. That baby will judge our works, save or discard our accumulated goods, and judge our books as worthy or unworthy of keeping. That baby will perpetuate or destroy our dreams.

Few of the world's old hopes will die when we die, but it will have many new hopes born with every child who comes to life. Let us then welcome the baby's invasion with eagerness, and anticipate it with ample preparation. Let us provide for the baby the warmth, the closeness, the intimacy, and the understanding essential to true security and the freedom essential to personal fufillment. Let us provide the discipline needed for noble becoming and the example needed for lofty guidance. Someday we will see the invasion was truly life's great hour.

We shall see what will become
of his dreams.

GENESIS 37:20

CHAPTER FIVE

Dreams Need to Grow Too

The broidered path to the marriage altar passes through a mystic woodland of dreaming. Dreams sing like birds from the branches of trees; they whisper from brooks and waterfalls and gentle breezes. Hope blossoms like a rainbow hue of flowers beside the path. Splendid aspirations float like strains of Mendelssohn or Beethoven across the dawning loveliness of every shared pathway. Courting is a time for reaching eagerly into the mystic morrows and building splendid castles there. To be in love is to be afire with beautiful intentions. The mating couple whose courtship becomes

96

only a time of seeing each other's physical attractiveness rather than the beauty of each other's aspirations will but bring together two lovely animal-beings and stifle their soul-life.

The courtship in which no great new dreams are conceived is of the flesh only. Separate even the prettiest girl from her loftiest golden intentions and you have robbed her of something indispensable to noble womanhood. Separate even the most handsome, capable man from his finest ambitions and you have left but the hulk of him. The life without dreams is destined to early dullness and emptiness. Even the most handsome couple is approaching early ugliness if their altar-bound dreams do not include more than physical license. If only the flesh is wed, there is little material for building a home.

Marriage mates must not only look mutually after the physical needs and safety of each other, but they must be prepared to protect, defend, and cultivate the dreams of their mates as well. Only in man did the Creator invest the Godlike capacity to create, to invent, to think of, and want that which could not be seen. Early in life the eager spirit of a person begins to grope into the unknown and the unseen and build there the ideas and assets of life. A small boy sprawls on his back beneath the apple tree and watches through the branches the soft clouds overhead. His racing young mind begins to people the sky with splendid creations of which he is a noble part. A girl, quite young, begins to look out her window at the stars and to "wish upon a star" for things which are as yet entirely out of sight.

How close is the person to God when he or she is dreaming of pure, worthy, holy things! Of course marriage is part of that pattern of dreaming. It is a step of faith into the unmarked future, "for better or for worse—till death us do part." It is dreams rising above the cluttering ruins which blotch the community and spread sorrow across the countryside. Dreams are never altogether safe unless they are kindled by fellowship with the Creator. Marriage is a lovely adventure when based on such a soul-born experience.

A girl's dreams must include orange blossoms but also flower gardens, pretty curtains, homey furniture, and comfortable living. She must dream of giving her finest self to a husband and children. Regardless of how lofty her aspirations in some professional career, she should never marry without comparable desires to be a good wife and mother.

A young man coming to the marriage altar needs the eager excitement of a dream he will hold softly in his arms, clothed in lace and satin, but he must also have those rugged, sturdy dreams which will push him resolutely into a productive career. His dream must be able to make him knuckle down to hard work, self-sacrifice, and personal discipline. A man who has accomplished his major purpose when he gets a girl to marry him does not have much of a goal to set his life by.

Proposing to a Dream

Before two people give serious consideration to marriage they should be sufficiently acquainted to know each other's inner aspirations. They should never allow their acquaintance to become more than a good friendship if their dreams are not sufficiently compatible to be possible of fulfillment in the same home. A girl who dreams of being a missionary and a boy who aspires to take over his father's business are in for trouble if they marry. The two dreams cannot live in the same house and one must suffer slow, miserable death for the sake of the other. A young man who dreams of entering the ministry and a young lady who aspires to be an actress should face up to the hard facts of life before they become too involved in each other's lives. The young man who hopes to be a farmer will be foolish if he proposes marriage to a girl whose whole ambition is rooted in city life.

In no other area is the mating of dreams more relevant than in the moral and religious aspirations. The young woman who dreams of a Christian home, an active church life, a wide church association, and religious rituals in the family should not consider marriage to a young man who is not interested in these. Even though he may promise to tolerate these things, he will be unable to enter heartily into them because they are not basically part of his dream. He may industriously and faithfully follow his ambition in some professional field and be very successful as a material provider, but her dream will slowly disintegrate. Something in her own heart will die.

What Happens When a Dream Dies? If the marriage of two people would mean the stifling and death of the dreams of either, it could not possibly be more than half a marriage and would result in frustration for both persons. For a person to have to live with the resentments of unborn dreams is folly. Even the one whose dream appears to survive will be handicapped by the fact that life must be lived with the mate who has been forced to give up so much for it. A truly good person will find it difficult to enjoy personal success while loving a person whose equally meaningful aspiration is being slowly put to death. Incompatible dreams will produce, at best, a mediocre marriage.

Some people come to marriage without any aspiration sufficiently well formed to make a difference. Their small dreams can easily be adapted to those they have learned to love. Truly big dreams seldom come this late in life, but slowly maturing people may begin to dream when they begin to love and by the very nature of things will evolve aspirations which conform to those of the persons they marry.

There are people who are so busy with little dreams that they have no time for big ones. Many girls are so busy with dreams of being a bride that they never dream of being a housewife, and some are so starry-eyed over a wedding that they give little thought to a marriage. Some young men have no dreams beyond apparent horizon where their love and the love of a pretty girl are consummated in a wedding. What a rude awakening they will have when they find that beyond that horizon stretches most of life with all its hard reality and ruggedness!

Marriage consummated by two people whose dreams are compatible should give birth to new and nobler aspirations involving both of them. As with their physical offspring, their jointly conceived dreams will contain a little of both, which will give even greater dimension to them. For a husband and wife one of the highest objectives is to be congenially mated. If so, their careers as well as their home will be mutually enriched. A marriage which simply unites two people in bondage to the routine of daily living is a failure. If all they do is work, pay bills, sleep, eat, and raise a family, they are destined to live a dull life indeed.

Young people are totally unfitted for marriage until they have a well-defined plan for their future. They must have something in mind which is so demanding and lofty that it will call forth their best. It must demand sacrifice, devotion, and hard work. If it doesn't, they will probably quit learning, quit adventuring, and quit preparing for anything beyond their trip home from work one day at a time. A high proportion of marriages consummated by young people who have not yet settled upon a life purpose will fail within a few years, or the parties accept the docile contentment of mediocrity. Likewise, people who bear children in a home where there are no vital parental aspirations will condemn that new generation to a life of drugery and ugliness. Children need from their parents the stimulation of dreams as well as the strengthening of food.

Noble Dreams Are Marriageable. A man who dreams of success in the field of law or medicine, for example, and a woman who dreams of success primarily in the field of homemaking, motherhood, and related areas should have no difficulty in helping each other reach their goals. Surely no woman can have a nobler dream than that which finds self-fulfillment in the making of a home.

Along with her dreams of homemaking she may aspire to a secondary field in art, music, or writing. This may be quite compatible with the dream of her husband. If on the other hand her dreams of the fine arts take precedence over her homemaking goal, she should not marry a man whose life needs the fulfillment of a pleasant home companionship.

No person can know genuine personal fulfillment without the experience of seeing some dreams come true. The very experience of aspiring is good, but if it is robbed of any rewarding achievement it tends to become frustrating. When two persons marry, they should know that their future happiness depends very much upon their ability to help each other achieve their goals.

Fulfillment in housekeeping and homemaking is a project in which the aspiring husband should ardently help his mate. He should not only provide finance without humiliation, gifts, and material equipment, but he should take an interested part in helping her about the house, helping with the children, and being involved in the whole family experience. If she has secondary ambitions toward the fine arts, he should help her attain these things. A wife who finds fulfillment in writing a book or painting a picture should enjoy the husband's blessing upon her efforts. The achievement

101

of the secondary goal often has to be deferred during the years of childbearing and baby tending. But this can be one of enriching and revitalizing experiences of later life. Even though the dream must wait, however, it should never be allowed to die.

The Changing World of Men and Women

Today, marriage is being forced to contend with much more intermingling of the sexes than in previous years. A few years back male and female employees usually worked separately and in differing fields. Few women were employed in public places, and when they were it was not likely that male employees would be working side by side with them. The women talked with other women employees, the men with the men, and there was little social exposure between them. Today with one-third of the labor force being women, we find the picture radically changed. Men and women work side by side in offices, factories, professions, and careers. They become good friends, talk shop, discuss their work mutually, and come to know each other's lives more personally than before.

Today a woman attorney may freely join the men at the bar association luncheon while her husband is having luncheon with the women who teach in the same school as he. A woman in one area of a factory may eat in one lunchroom with other women and men while the man working elsewhere eats in another lunchroom with other men and women. Men and women salespeople work together in the store quite like a large family. A husband may be part of such a group in one store and the wife shares those experiences in a store across town. It is very possible that a secretary may have to spend more time with her boss than she is able to spend with her husband. In such complicated patterns as these days present, the marriage partners must give special attention to the cultivation of their

102

homelife. What hours they have together must be cherished and filled with the most meaningful experiences.

Career Dreams for Married People. This new situation makes possible many career openings to women which a few years ago only men could apply for. This change is not all bad nor is it all good. But whether we like it or not, we cannot change the situation. It simply means that each must be given room to dream and to aspire in these areas without arousing the jealousy of a marriage partner. This new freedom must be maintained with such integrity and honesty as to give no cause for mistrust or suspicion. This is not easy for insecure or immature people. Marriage mates must be prepared to live lives utterly loyal to each other in the midst of a situation where associations with a great many other men and women are commonplace and are accepted. The fact that a man works beside women all day does not give him the least excuse for undue familiarity, and the fact that a woman sees her boss more hours in the day than she sees her husband need not in the least divert her from complete fascination with her marriage partner. At least it had better not!

Cultivation of the Marriage Dream. People who cease to be proud of each other will cease to dream together. A very important factor in the new employment pattern is the need of husbands and wives to make their best possible appearance at home. The wife who is always well-dressed when she goes to work and is busy all day around a well-dressed, neatly shaved boss should be able to come home to a well-shaved, neatly dressed, and genteel man. If the man to whom she comes home is slovenly, grouchy, and disagreeable, the comparison cannot but be damaging. The man who works all day around secretaries who are nicely dressed, well-educated, and gracious-mannered should not need to come home at night and meet a woman with uncombed hair, a nagging voice, and a completely dis-organized life.

The only way marriage partners can be sure to keep a spouse proud today is by outdoing the competition. They cannot fight it. Efforts to do so will but undo their cause. They must continually rise to the occasion and be prepared to offer so much of interest, love, inspiration, and intimacy at home that a weary spouse will be eager for quitting time so that the home companionship can be enjoyed. Wives must be careful to keep up their appearance at home. They must look attractive, speak winsomely, and maintain a high demand for themselves in the minds and hearts of their husbands. Husbands must be interesting. They must be honorable and princely, gracious and well-mannered —so much so that when they arrive at home their wives will find them a refreshing change from the men they have seen all day at the job.

Dreams Should Have a Timetable. Love must not be allowed to completely disorganize the timetable of dreams. First of all, young people should have some dreams for the future which must come ahead of marriage. Marriage should not be so hurried as to interrupt young people's preparation for life. No person is ready for marriage until he has a well-defined plan for life. Well-disciplined people will fit their marriage date into their educational program. They will not defeat their long-range plans by reason of eagerness to possess each other. It is better that they withhold themselves from each other long enough that when they come together they will be prepared for making the most of life. Millions of people have crippled their dreams by hasty marriages. They intended to go on and finish their educations but found too late that educations do not come easily while rearing a family.

Sometimes a timetable for dreams will mean that with mutual consent one person will postpone the realization of his or her personal dream until the other is given first chance. It is often necessary for the time-table to put one ahead of the other but it should not be that one is completely sacrificed for the other. The young woman whose major dream is motherhood and family rearing may find it best that she wait for part of her own fulfillment until her husband gets his edu-cation. However, he should not ask her dream to wait too long nor defer it until his own plans are completely fulfilled. He should include a timetable for her dreams too.

There will be times when one must hold up a dream until the other gets within reach of fulfillment, but there should be the full reciprocation of effort until both know the adventure of fulfilled lives.

Some dreams should be on the caldendar for the early years of marriage, some should come in later adult life, and some should be waiting for fulfillment in old age. There should always be dreams in creation. No barren eras are necessary in life.

Dreams become quite meaningless if we do nothing to fulfill them. It is easy to allow them to dissipate like the mist of morning. Most people who are failures in life are those who had great dreams and plans but failed to demand of themselves the disciplines necessary to reach their goals.

Aspirations must be tough, durable things. They must be capable of staying alive while buried for years under clutter and confusion. They must be able to sur-vive illness and disappointment. They must outlive our frustrations and remain intact when badly shaken. No person is bigger than his dreams and none can survive as a complete person longer than his aspirations keep him fully alive. No life is boring until its dreaming is done. He who still aspires is not a victim of drudgery. So long as there is a brisk flame in the soul there will be a light in the life. He who is genuinely in love with the stars will never bemoan the nights nor become panicked by the gathering dark.

Dreams Must Be Subject to Enlargement and Addition. In the pioneering country when young couples married they would build a small cottage in which to make their home, but they always constructed it so that a room could be added when a baby came. As time went on, room after room would be added, and though the architectural pattern was nothing to brag about, the utility of it was unique. A house to which no rooms could be added was for old people.

In a wholesome marriage new dreams and aspirations, hopes and ambitions will develop. New interests will appear and new opportunities will arise. How fortunate are those people who are emotionally, physically, and mentally capable of these enlarging experiences.

The Finest Dreams Are in Becoming, Not in Getting. No young couple should allow themselves merely to aspire to owning things or buying things. People whose hopes are dependent upon money and what money can buy, success and what success can give, or power and what power can bring are on thin ice. We do not always have control of these things, and the most able workmen often find themselves deprived of material success.

It is better to dream of becoming a painter than of owning a Picasso. It is better to dream of learning to play the piano than of owning an elaborate library of music. It is better to aspire to become a good workman than to be able to purchase things other workmen have made.

He who strives to become an author aspires more loftily than he who merely dreams of owning a great library. The woman who becomes able to make her own clothes will find more enjoyment than she who gets rich enough to buy them freely. The family which learns to enjoy gardening will relish vegetables more than those who merely learn how to shop for the best. The joy of becoming something is always more excellent than the joy of possessing something.

People who spend their lives and their strength trying to own a big house rather than striving to be people who make a happy home are robbing themselves.

Children Should Live and Grow in a Garden of Dreams. No child has a chance in life if enclosed in a house where dreams give no windows on the world. Children must be taught that they can become anything they set out to become. They should be taught to aim high and have the utmost confidence that they can make it. On the other hand they should never be taught that things come easy or that life will hand them opportunities, advantages, or immunities. Children should learn to form and perpetuate their dreams in a very earthy and severe world. They should see their parents continually learning, aspiring, and becoming something finer. They should themselves be aiming at something bigger. They should have the assurance that they *can* do things and should have confidence in their skill and ability to perform tasks which are within their reach. They should not be taught to fear life nor be skeptical of people. No child should be shielded from bumps at the expense of his aspirations nor be forbidden to climb so that he becomes earthbound for life. Of course every child needs the protection and prudence of parental guidance and must be shielded from the sure suicide which results from childish foolishness and daring, but their belief in themselves and their devotion to their dreams should not be stifled.

Parents should share their dreams with their children from the first so that the children can share the interest and help reach toward the fulfillment of them. The children should be taught to freely discuss their dreams with their parents. The little boy who takes turns at wanting to become a fireman, a cowboy, a prizefighter, and a ditchdigger should not be belittled or made fun of. It is better simply to expose the child to finer things, and as a growing mind reaches out a wise choice will be made. If his first expression of aspiration is ridiculed, it is likely he will begin to smother his ambitions rather than to talk of them.

Secondhand Dreams Won't Fit Comfortably. We humans are likely to be so impressed with our own dreams that we think everybody else should be equally impressed. A wife who is sure of the soundness of her goals may find resentment or unconcern when she tries to make her husband equally interested. It may be difficult for him to wear her dreams comfortably. Sometimes a wife dreams of her husband being a banker while the man she marries dreams more fittingly of being a carpenter. She may be so insistent that she tries to press him into the mold of her dream. This might on rare occasions be successful but it is so unlikely as to be a dangerous practice. If the wife wants to be a musician it is unlikely that a husband's dream of her being an author will become a satisfactory transplant. Transplanted dreams seldom live and grow.

Parents obsessed with some vision for their children may force them to follow a path that they do not wish to take. This is an injustice. A boy may want to farm while his mother dreams of him being a lawyer. The mother might keep pressing for her way until the boy tries to fulfill her dream but it is almost sure to be a disappointment to them both. The girl may want to marry and enjoy a career as homemaker and mother while her mother is convinced that she should have a career in music. The mother may force her will on the daughter for a long time and find it utterly miserable for all concerned. The father who dreams so intently of the boy taking over his business may do injury to a boy who feels an inner call to the ministry. Dreams are very personal things and should never be imposed upon another. Parents should teach their children to dream their own dreams rather than teaching them to re-dream an unfulfilled dream of the parent.

Sometimes parents whose lives have proved disappointing and whose dreams lie in shambles try to re-create an opportunity for their dream to be realized by superimposing it upon their child. The result is frustration to both. The child needs guidance and every possible maturing experience, but let the choice of a career and the kindling of a dream be his own. This attempt at extension of a parental aspiration often is a problem with grandparents as well as parents, and many a child has been pressed into an ill-fitting mold by the dominant will of grandparents who insist on the child supporting a reincarnation of their life ambition.

Some Less Colorful Dreams Are the More Rewarding. The woman who chooses the career of motherhood and whose loftiest ambition is to give the world children who are adequate and wholesome is choosing the finest dream on earth. It may seem less exciting to some people, for it is involved in scrubbing and mopping, cleaning and cooking. It is a daily routine of changing diapers on babies, running errands, and sewing on buttons. She cannot dress as well about her work as does the business and professional woman but that does not mean that her career is less rewarding. The truth is that for women this career produces probably the finest sense of fulfillment and the richest heritage of love of any. When a woman is old and feeble and life's last pages are fluttering before the evening winds, nothing is so rewarding as the visit of a grandchild, a letter from a distant son, or a strong young arm around feeble shoulders. In hours like that the memory of a name on an office door, a prominent desk in the office, a large bank account, or a large wardrobe seems very cold and meaningless.

Whatever career a woman chooses and whatever her dreams, there should be no dream so colorful as to take her attention away from motherhood. If she can be a mother first and a career woman last, she may find the new freedoms provided for women quite interesting.

Senior Citizens Should Still Dream

Never has there been a time when the lives of so many people were extended beyond the working years as now. On the one hand science continues to add years to our life expectancy, while at the same time people are retiring earlier. The result is a long eventide of life which can become desperately tedious. The person whose dreams were all involved in hard work and had their genius in the productive years will find that these added years become a burden. How disappointing to conclude a busy life with ten, twenty, or thirty years which are empty of meaning and barren of purpose! No one should resign himself to being merely towed in on the home stretch, but should keep his engines running and his wheels turning.

To have too many years left after the end of our dreaming is worse than having "too much month left at the end of the money." There must be some provision for rekindling the inner flame of people whose first series of goals have either been reached or have ceased to be a possibility.

Dreams in old age are made of the stuff collected throughout life. Nobody can wait until retirement to get ready for it. The persons we become through the first sixty years of life are the persons we will live with very intimately from sixty until seventy, eighty, or ninety. If the persons we become are unhappy and dull, it is sure that our eventide companionship with ourselves will be disappointing and dismal.

People must prepare a dream for old age—such as some useful service in the church, the community, the Sunday school, or work with boys and girls. Throughout their lifetime people should plan ahead and enrich old age by qualifying themselves for service to others and to God. The mind must be kept alive. Of course it won't be quite as alert in later life as in early life, but if people memorize good materials in childhood they will be greatly enriched for old age.

People should learn to enjoy little things close at hand. It may be that when they are old they cannot afford orchids, but if they have learned to see some loveliness in a dandelion they will not be too impoverished. There will always be plenty of interesting things in the world for the people who keep interested in life's parade of little things. From such a resource life can maintain sparkling interest until the very last.

Learn the Joy of Serving Others. Throughout active life people will have to spend the major amount of their time working at their jobs and performing earthy duties. Plans for later years should include time to do things for the mere sake of being helpful, and giving oneself simply for the joy of giving. What a thrill it is to have something of self to give away!

Keep the materials for dreaming. The people among whom the eager years are spent become the very fabric of happy living in later years. The person who moves away from old friends is moving away from most of the substance for dreams. He is too old to form a large number of new friendships or to share a great number of experiences with many new people. Only under the most demanding conditions should older people move from the community where their vigorous years have been invested.

111

Hobbies Should Become Serious Business. Fishing, camping, gardening, painting, music, or a hundred other things offer outlets for the people whose lives are mostly yesterday. Letter writing, visiting friends, reading, and other things which the busy years made impossible or limited, should be enjoyed now. It doesn't take a lot of money but it does take ingenuity and courage to keep dreaming when life is nearly over, and it surely makes a beautiful sunset for the ending of the day.

Life is not long for any of us but its area can be increased only by adding width to its short span. The person whose dreams kindle great aspirations through the years will find a broad area of enjoyment at the end. Old age is after all only the accumulated becoming, the gathered attainments, and the total of the experiences of the years gone before. That man and woman who had the good fortune to be reared in childhood homes where they were taught to dream, and who have kept their dreams aglow until the sunset of life, will know the true satisfaction of self-fulfillment.

Houses, palaces, or mansions can be bought or built by those with gold at hand, but a wholesome marriage can develop within those walled spaces only when dreams, as well as bodies, grow therein. What romance flowers when dreams are developing! What fragrance fills the environment when love is blessed with eager hopes! When aspirations wed at the marriage altar, they go forth to multiply and replenish the earth.

Let us not be alarmed by the fantastic ambitions of a child but rather be frightened if these should give way to things too small. Be not shocked by the staggering size of the plans of youth, but rather be disturbed if youth dreams of puny, easily reached goals. Do not be amazed at the outlandish size of a man's aspirations, but be shocked by the inclination of society to pour cold water on his waking fires. Do not think it inordinate that old men should see visions or dream dreams, for they are enriched by all the accumulated wisdom of years and have the material for the loftiest goals of all. Old age brings us into possession of life's full heritage, and two people who have dreamed together through the hurrying seasons should revel in a wealth of new enchantments.

> *You must be merciful, as your Father*
> *in Heaven is merciful. Don't judge*
> *other people and you will not be judged*
> *yourselves. Don't condemn and you will not*
> *be condemned. Make allowances for others*
> *and people will make allowances for you.*
> —LUKE 6:36-37*

CHAPTER SIX

When a Marriage Becomes Ill

Marriages, like individuals, can become ill. Just as some persons are more inclined to illness than others, so marriages vary in their susceptibility to breakdown.

The marriage which is basically not strong will need special care throughout its lifetime. It can, however, be completely satisfying and rewarding when proper care is given to it. Even the marriage which is basically robust and least allergic to irritating environments will have some share of hardships and

*New Testament in Modern English, © J. B. Phillips, 1958. Used by permission of the Macmillan Company.

pains. There is no marriage which is immune to misfortunes and ailments. If any home is to be lastingly happy it will be kept that way by due diligence and healthful habits.

Some marriages are consummated by people who are already emotionally, physically, or morally ill, and their illness cannot be so isolated as to prevent it affecting the marriage. Personality illness in one member of the marriage team will make the marriage ill.

Marriages however, like people, are subject to treatment and cure. If people will be realistic and sensible about their marital problems, there are very few incurable ailments. The trouble is usually magnified by the fact that the involved persons are so reluctant to acknowledge these problems. People who are quite free to discuss their physical weaknesses or afflictions will hide their marital problems as though they had committed a crime. People who will go quickly to a doctor in case of bodily ailments will refuse to seek professional aid when a marriage is in trouble. In most cases, the people whose home and marriage are in serious trouble will put off any appeal for outside help until there is little chance of recovery. The sooner help is sought and treatment is begun, the more likely the ailing marriage is to be recoverable.

If ailing marriages could be cured by the use of medicines, surgery, or manipulation applied by a doctor there would be a much better recovery rate. People do not hesitate to place their physical problems in the hands of an expert and bear the pain of having the doctor operate on them or give them pills. If the doctor, however, simply tells them to change their habits, cultivate new routines, change their diets, or discipline themselves more strictly, a great many will fall down.

In the treatment of ailing marriages nothing can be done by pills and purgatives. It must be done with

115

disciplines, and this causes the process to be less appealing and interesting. Yet, with so much involved, a person stands to gain more by obedience to the prescribed disciplines in curing a marriage illness than in curing a physical ailment. No person can be fully happy, no life can be genuinely full, and no success can be fully enjoyed if the marriage relation is painful.

There Are Ailments Peculiar to Each Age. Not all of the ailments of our bodies are common to all ages. Some diseases are known as children's diseases, some are diseases more common to young adulthood, some to middle life, and some are common to people late in life. So with marriage problems. The newly married are more likely to have one set of problems; the fifteen-year-, the twenty-five-year-, and the fifty-year-old marriages, each in turn, are subject to differing sets of problems. As with physical disease, there is no absolute definition, so that sometimes an old person gets the chicken pox and sometimes a young person gets arthritis. So with marriages. Some old marriages develop problems usually associated with young homes and vice versa.

The very young marriage—that is, one consummated in the late teens—is definitely exposed to problems having to do with immaturity. There is the matter of insufficient self-discipline, uncontrolled spending habits, inclination to quit a project when it loses its first excitement, and various other carry-overs from childhood. We do not often find a major problem building up around the sex life of these very young marriages because of their emotional abandon, their physical eagerness, and their vigorous bodily activity. However, we do find that financial problems and economic pressures are very often acute. Only the finest training and the best of personal disciplines can keep such marriages happy.

This group, likewise, is more susceptible to the problems growing out of parental interference. Parents are more likely to try to help these very young people, and of all people who do not want parental interference, it is they. Many times they have actually married hastily to escape the authority of Mother or Father, and to find that in marriage they have not only mothers but mothers-in-law is quite a shock.

The boy and girl planning to marry in their late teens should be prepared to have a hard row to hoe. It is difficult to make a go of life in the face of the many difficult situations. There is financial hardship amounting at times to actual physical hunger; there is shortage of clothing which becomes actually humiliating. Adult responsibilities are for adults to bear, and marriage is for adults. For a person in the late teens to step into the irreversible situations of adulthood will demand some very courageous self-discipline.

The fact that so many who marry young take that step as an escape from authority or discipline and many others precipitate themselves into it by undisciplined sexual activity means that this age-group includes many people who are predestined to hardship. People who seek escapes in life or who lack self-command will be susceptible to marital illnesses as long as they live unless they establish new disciplines.

Marriages consummated in the mid-twenties are on the average the most healthy. The parties to these marriages are usually well-educated; they have had social experiences on a wider scale by having individually dated numerous people of the opposite sex. They are financially in position to support their marriage wholesomely and are generally better prepared for the experiences of adulthood. They are usually persons who have developed sufficient self-discipline to make marriage congenial. This is not always true, however.

Illness in such marriages, if it does come, is more

likely to be found in areas of religious differences, differences in cultural patterns or in economic prudence. In case children come in rapid succession to such a couple it is sometimes difficult for them to adjust to the new captivity imposed by parenthood after their brief years of greater social and physical liberty.

Marriages entered into in middle or later life are susceptible to a varying pattern of diseases and problems. Many of these are related to factors of health, social attitudes, personal habits, etc.

Marriage Is for the Entire Life-span. The normal marriage must endure through the exposures of every age-group from young adulthood to old age and must encounter the problems, be exposed to the diseases, and experience the hazards contingent to every changing situation. Just as the problems are actually closely related, so the remedies are sufficiently basic as to justify a few simple rules of treatment.

The couple who learn early in their married life to diagnose symptoms and to cope with their illnesses will likely handle them successfully through life. Those persons who cannot seem to learn by experience and must encounter each new situation unprepared will live in perpetual tensions and troubles.

All Big Illnesses Start with Small Irritations. Every disease is best treated before it reaches major proportions. If people detect the presence of a problem early and take immediate steps to correct it, they usually save themselves major suffering. The trouble becomes serious when a couple let the plague get too big a start. They wait until the misery of it is intolerable before beginning to look for a cure. Most marital unhappiness could be avoided if the couple would mutually go to work on their irritations the moment they are discovered.

If the treatment can be applied and the problem

worked out before communication between the two is broken, there is every chance for success. However, when the circulation or communication is clogged, treatment and recovery are greatly hindered. Good, free, and open communications between the two parties to the marriage are the most important factor in establishing and maintaining marital health. Once this is inhibited, the disease will linger long. After the ability to talk things over together is lost, treatment is more difficult, though cure is still very possible.

THERAPY FOR AN AILING MARRIAGE

1. *Recognize a Problem When It Appears.*

The problem may be simply a trifling incident arising over an unimportant matter, but if it tends to fester and become inflamed, there is more to it than the eruption. Every couple will and should have differences of opinion. This is wholesome. But if those differences begin to wedge them apart, the situation is serious. Usually the occasion which appears to be the issue in such cases is only a symptom and the actual cause is something more basic. No disease is quickly cured by simply treating the symptom. The disease itself should be treated.

There is usually a reason why people are difficult and contentious. Merely getting them to apologize for what they did will not correct the matter. If one keeps a secret from the other, the matter of the secret is not so important as what caused him to keep it. The fact that one nags is not so much the problem as what causes the nagging. These things are usually symptoms rather than the basic disease. Treating symptoms is never sufficient.

2. *Be Willing to Apply Self-discipline.*

The person who would correct a home problem must first of all begin to work with himself or herself.

People seldom accomplish much if they try to correct the faults in another without admitting or going to work on their own. Our Lord was so right when He advised people to remove the beams from their own eyes before attempting to remove the splinters from the eyes of others! Until people are sufficiently concerned and humbled to go more than half of the way themselves, there is little reason to hope for effective treatment.

A wise marriage counselor will not sit with a complaining member of a marriage pair and go over the faults of the absent member with the thought of correcting the absent person. Treatment and corrective measures must start with the one who is willing to bend first, to accept self-discipline, and to make some adjustments. It is not uncommon to find that a very good person makes a less good spouse. Sometimes a genuinely good, Christian spouse, who is deeply religious and sincerely dedicated, is still difficult to live with. Sometimes even goodness can be made offensive to an ungodly spouse by the mere expedient of always including God on one side of every issue. God is not always in hearty approval of the acts of basically godly people nor is He always opposed to everything done by a basically ungodly person. The most religious people sometimes must eat humble pie, and the best of marriage partners must remember that they too may be in the wrong about many things.

Very few marriage problems would be insoluble if both persons would willingly go to work on their own faults first. It is not often, however, that both will undertake this step simultaneously. If corrective measures are found they are usually found first by an intensely concerned spouse and by self-discipline on the part of that one. The pressures begin to be reduced so that eventually the other sees the possibility of something being accomplished and begins to cooperate from the other side.

Almost never is an ailing marriage restored to health so long as either or both husband and wife are trying to correct the other rather than themselves. Other people are not corrected that way. Love which will go a second mile, and a third, and a tenth will work best.

3. *Watch Out for Little Irritations.*

The decay in marital happiness begins with rather trifling things. However, when even a trifling thing becomes multiplied by repetition or joined by numerous other irritations it makes for serious attrition upon the marriage. It is not a serious thing for a man to track mud into the house, provided it is not a repeated practice. It is not a serious thing for him to leave his clothes strung all over the house, provided it is not a daily practice. However, if such things are repeated day after day and if the man allows the kind and number of these irritating things to increase, he will become less welcome about the house. The marriage suffers, even if it is not destroyed.

One of the most irritating family problems is commonly known as nagging. It is not so much in what is said as in how and how often it is said. Sometimes this comes of a parental home environment and needs correction by self-discipline. Often it is the outcropping expression of inner tensions which develop in the marriage.

Sometimes the nagging habit develops in the home as an unconscious defiance of personality submergence. If one marriage partner dominates the other to where frank sharing is impossible, the one who feels suppressed can and often does resort to repeated small, jabbing words. Against this the dominating mate has no defense and if the cause is not corrected the symptom will increase.

Many wives resort to nagging as an undefined, un-recognized effort to keep the husband at a distance be-cause of tensions in the marital sex life. In some cases the husbands are not sufficiently thoughtful in pro-tecting their wives against unwanted pregnancy. The wife, finding herself too heavily burdened by babies coming too frequently, resorts to nagging as a defense mechanism. The wife would not boldly refuse her hus-band's affection nor his endearments, but deep within her the resentments express themselves in repeatedly calling the husband's attention to even his most trivial mistakes. It is an unspoken, unrecognized effort to keep him back. In such cases the pair should deliberately and kindly be frank about their problem. If such in-security is plaguing the wife, they should make her protection a mutual concern and by wholesome, health-ful means allay her fears.

These irritations gradually infect the entire marriage relationship. The cause as well as the symptom must be treated lest it eventually destroy communi-cation. If they continue there is diminishing of mutual love, there are more unkind words, there is less respect for the wishes and interests of each other, and the romance slowly withers on the vine. Eventually there is less tenderness, fewer caresses, and less show of affection on the part of one or both. By this time easy communication between the two is gone and restoration is difficult and slow.

Many couples seem to think that sexual incompat-ability is the basis of their marital tensions. They over-look the fact that such a situation is usually the result of other tensions, and if the tensions had been removed at the first there would have been greater enjoyment for both partners for life. Many try to correct the condition by trying to find medical stimulants, new techniques, emotional pressures, and other means which are unnatural. They forget that the sexual intimacy of marriage is the normal expression of affection and love. It is the result of two people wanting very much to be together, to give themselves to each other, and to belong to each other. It is the pinnacle of expressed devotion. It is a mountaintop which is arrived at by the paths of happy living, and when it is treated as a duty rather than as a fulfillment there is trouble.

When the intimate relationships of marriage are treated only as a means of physical outlet and animal expression, the marriage is well on the way to decay. Intimacy cannot be forced nor demanded without becoming repugnant. Intimacy must be created by all the processes which lead up to it normally and romantically. Without a doubt there are times when physical factors enter in and when there is a genuine human barrier to mutual enjoyment but these are rare. In such cases a doctor should be consulted. However, most of the problems in this area of marriage arise from habits and attitudes which originate through carelessness about things thought trifling. The first step toward correcting this marital illness is to correct the things which produced it and be willing to experience a long period of recultivation before expecting a complete cure. It can be done and it is worth a thousand times the effort and time involved.

4. *Beware of Jealousy.*

Jealousy is one of the most vicious and difficult conditions which can invade a marriage. It is sometimes produced by a professedly broad-minded spouse taking undue liberties. If prior to marriage one of the pair has lived in a home where the parents played and socialized quite intimately with other married couples, where they put their arms thoughtlessly about other married people of the opposite sex and jested freely about and with each other, it is likely that the young person will carry into marriage the idea that this is the way married people normally act. If the other young spouse came from a home where dignity ruled, where reserve was kept, and where such activities were frowned upon, it will be very difficult for that young marriage partner to avoid an unpleasant attitude when the spouse behaves as his or her parents behaved. The only way to correct this situation in the new home will be for a new standard to be formed which is sufficiently reserved to be inoffensive to both. It is unwise for either mate to be too suspicious, too reserved, or too afraid, but on the other hand it is extremely dangerous for either of them to be too free with people of the opposite sex and still hope to maintain a happy home.

If a young husband is going to be putting his arms around other women, and a young wife is going to flirt with other men, they are asking for trouble. Even if both of them welcome that kind of liberty and are equally free to make a lively party out of social occasions, they are still heading for trouble. Eventually the practice will go too far and somebody will become furiously jealous. If jealousy has crept into the marriage, it will do no good to merely fight it by saying there is no cause for it. The thing to do is to correct the situation which produced it.

One of the frequent causes of jealousy is the marriage of an insecure person to a mate of whom he feels a bit unworthy. Jealousy thrives when a person marries someone considerably better-looking, better-educated, or better-situated than he. The insecure person fears his or her ability to hold to the good catch amid all the high-powered competition which surrounds the couple. The result often is a defensiveness which tries to fight off the competition, hold the spouse close to home, watch every move, and guard against the least invasion of friendliness by any person who could compete. This is a deadly attitude, for it becomes untrusting, ugly, and unhappy so that the unfortunate spouse finds no joy at home but is chained close to home by an untrusting mate.

The way to fight jealousy is to outdo the competition. The person who sets out to simply give more than the competition could offer will have little difficulty. He or she may be unable to provide as handsome or pretty features as the competition, but a smile on the plainest features makes them wonderfully attractive. One may not have the fine figure possessed by others, but he can have the cleanest, most attractive, and most desirable personality of all. If a spouse picked a mate out of the entire crowd, then that spouse can be kept by making the best possible use of the qualities at hand.

Jealousy which tries to solve its problems by working on the other person directly will fail. Insecure persons should go to work on themselves and work on what they have and are until they have no reason for insecurity. If any spouse finds that his or her freedom with the other sex outside the home is creating jealousy, that situation should be corrected at once. Such unwise liberties are not only offensive to the marriage partner but they are likely to be the downfall of a person who feels very sure of self-control.

5. Don't Let Work Destroy the Home.

No home can survive without employment. There must be work invested to support the home financially and to keep the home physically. Work is a blessing. The couple who do not have to work are blighted with a bitter curse. Too much work will seldom hurt either a person or a marriage, but neglect of the home and marriage will destroy even the finest romance.

There must be time and strength reserved for each other. If a man works so much at the job that he is unable to be a pleasant mate at home, he must face up to the situation and make an adjustment. If a woman works so hard at keeping the house that she has no liveliness left for being an interesting wife, she is making a mistake. Sometimes a couple need to sit down and restudy their whole pattern of work and play and make a radical change in their activity structure. If a couple's way of doing things now is eroding the romance from the marriage, they should take corrective action, not sit and hope for it to cure itself. Something should be changed.

If mealtimes are boring, they can be corrected. If the conversation at the table is either nil or irritating, something should be done about it. It is normal for people to enjoy their meals together. Mealtime conversation is as important as the food served and can be planned as carefully. A well-set table will help some homes. New dishes prepared and served interestingly will help pull some out of the doldrums. Good stories and interesting incidents saved up for telling at the table will help some. Soft music will do a lot for some homes. Whatever it is, people should seriously seek out the things which will make even a little contribution toward rebuilding the table-time fellowship. Living together needs to be fun, even for tired people.

6. *Laughter Is a Good Medicine.*

The way some folks live, one would think they believed laughter was only for public occasions. Many couples would forget that laughter was possible to them were it not for the times they hear each other laugh when among other people. Why should a man have to take his wife out visiting to hear her laugh? Why should a wife have to invite guests in order to hear her husband laugh? When a couple get to where they never laugh together without others to hear them, there is something wrong. Young people courting can find cause for laughter in even the most trifling things. They laugh just for each other over almost anything that comes along. Why should laughter be so much harder to come by when people are married? Laughing together heals many little wounds, relieves many tensions, and welds an association into an intimate fellowship.

7. *Confusion Can Run a Marriage to Death.*

There is a lot of difference between mere commotion and busyness. It is seldom that real busyness hurts a home. Busy people are usually happy and considerate. Confused, harried people allow their commotion to wear them out and enervate their marriages.

People who find their mornings a panic, getting the children off to school an ordeal, and getting the husband off to work on time a daily emergency, are going to rob their home of the quietness and orderliness it must have. If mealtimes are under a constant pressure to hurry, and bedtimes are an ordeal in fighting the day to a dying close, there should be something done about it. This is principally the fault of bad organization, bad habits, and disordered living. This makes a marriage sick and can destroy it.

Couples who find their marriage nest shaken by such disorder should study it systematically. Their rising time can usually be adjusted a bit to give more time in the morning. A very few minutes can make the difference between pressure and leisureliness. Sometimes the bedtime at night needs to be adjusted ahead a bit to give time for a bit more sleep, so that the entire family will be more ready for the new day. The planning of the morning meal, the individual assignments of duties among the family members, and habits of happiness at the breakfast table can work wonders. Some homes could have much more available time if clothes, washcloths, towels, and other morning essentials were kept orderly and in place, so that last-minute searches would not upset the routine. The family members who go to bed at night knowing what clothes they will wear in the morning will relieve the morning of many trifling but annoying decisions.

It is difficult to change just one portion of a bad habit. It is better to revamp the entire situation sufficiently to correct a large area of problem, thus solving many lesser problems in one big adjustment. In many homes this should include the beginning of regular church attendance, establishment of family prayer and devotional practices, paying tithes and offerings to the church, and a host of other things. Undertaking such significant changes will create a sufficient upheaval in the status quo as to make possible a correction of the numerous apparently lesser diseases which have infected the home and marriage.

Many marriages which have seemed hopelessly on the rocks, and in which many efforts at reconstruction have failed, have been wonderfully restored when the people quit trying to correct some minor patterns and wholeheartedly accepted Christ, became all-out, genuine Christians, joined the church, and became active in it. The secret was a radical change in their total life structure and a reorientation around something infinitely worthwhile. It is not uncommon to find such homes now among the happiest in the community. They could not correct their problem a little at a time but they could undergo a complete overhaul, not only of the home, but of their own attitudes.

8. *Mental Illness Creates Home Tensions.*

There are all kinds and proportions of mental ailments. Many times people have no one but themselves to blame for emotional and neurotic disturbances. Persistence in unwholesome attitudes, uncurbed selfishness, self-pity, and undue attention to ailments can sometimes cause deep-seated problems. Long-harbored resentments, jealousies, and grudges can upset a person. Physical problems sometimes reflect themselves in emotional and mental difficulties. On many occasions there is no obvious cause, yet the fact of mental illness is with us. Unfortunately, we do not always recognize the fact of illness and blame the irregular person rather than trying to understand and help him. All the blaming and scolding in the world will not correct a situation which demands understanding and sympathetic help. If there is any likelihood of illness it is best to ask for help from a dependable doctor as soon as possible. Other members of the family must be prepared for long periods of patience and kindness in the face of a very difficult trial. This kind of illness should be treated with the same kindness and helpfulness as we would treat an organic injury or disease. Mental illness is usually curable, but the support of the family members is more important in its treatment than in treating the usually recognized physical diseases.

9. *Healing Sometimes Demands Acceptance of a Second Choice.*

There are times in life when we must be willing to give up a specific and splendid dream and settle for something different if we are to have anything left of our homes and marriages.

Many times a young lady has married with a dream of a splendid future that the man she married was incapable of fulfilling. Even though he did his best and was basically a fine husband, he would never be the towering professional specialist which she wanted as a husband. If she insists on the dream without regard to the capacity of her husband, she will frustrate him as well as herself. She will have to settle for something he is capable of reaching. She will find it is much better to live happily with a mechanic than to live in tension with an attorney. It is better to be a member of a happy pair in a farm home than to be the wife of a frustrated man in the city.

Many a man marries a wife whom he thinks should give him a kind of cultural companionship, a flowering social life, and a circle of attention in the crowd, only to find that the girl he married prefers a home and children, housekeeping and gardening. She may be quite incapable of the "ivory tower" life in which he would like to place her. She may make him very happy if he can adjust his dream to a dimension she can occupy, but if he persists in demanding the impossible he will have to accept a tense home and an irritable mate.

Many times a home is strained to the breaking point when one of the children marries differently from the desires of the parents. They must accept a daughter-in-law or son-in-law which would, to say the least, not have been their first choice. They can either accept the situation or they can put their newly adult offspring in a tense situation and keep themselves in a difficult place for the rest of their lives. Every home and every marriage will have times when second choices must be moved up to first place and accepted as part of life. And many times we live to see that in the long run the second choice could well have been first anyway.

If the strain in the home is due to holding on to a decaying dream impossible of attainment, it is best to give it up and make room for new dreams. Accept the challenge of making a cathedral, maybe less ornate and of a different dimension, of the materials which are still available.

10. *Prayer Is a Healing Balm.*

People who overlook prayer as a therapy in ailing marriages are missing too much. Admittedly not all

Christians have happy homes and not all people who pray live congenially. In fact, some very religious people are hard to live with. The fact that people are Christians does not necessarily mean that they are devoid of faults. However, Christians who know the meaning and value of prayer have at hand a wonderful means of grace and healing.

When people pray with regard to a home problem, there should be some rules to follow. In the first place, it is never good to pray merely about the troublesome spouse. There is no merit in telling the all-knowing God about all the faults of the person whom you chose to marry. In fact, the more you tell the Lord about those faults, the more you will be impressed by them. It is much better to pray *for* people than to pray *about* them. The most rewarding experience in prayer is that of praying for God's grace and blessing upon your own life. One should pray that God will help him to correct his own faults, become more lovable and helpful, and in general make life easier for the difficult mate.

A Sick Marriage Is Sick People

There is nothing wrong with marriage as an institution, but when the involved individuals become ill, the marriage they have contracted becomes ill too. We cannot correct our situation by changing the institution of marriage; we can only change the persons who are married. Marriage will work wonderfully when it is contracted by two persons whose lives are adequate and wholesome and who live by the rules God has ordained.

God can help. He can make the marriage partners strong to bear their responsibilities. He can make them capable of changing their ineffective ways to effective ones. God must not be overlooked in the quest for a happier marriage. He cannot do our part for us nor can He be charged with responsibility for our situations, but He will help us become persons who are capable of being wholesome marriage partners.

Don't Smother. Marriage should become the setting for a true self-fulfillment of both husband and wife. If it develops that either person is being submerged and robbed of personality growth, steps should be taken to correct the matter. If the marriage life pattern is inhibiting growth and happiness rather than enhancing it, there is no time for delay in beginning treatment. No couple on earth has ever yet discovered and enjoyed the full experience which is latent in marriage. There is a wide horizon yet unexplored in even the most effective marriage.

Some couples take possession of such a small area that they find it unable to support them happily and they starve out. Some occupy an area large enough for tolerable living and endure their homestead in a limited measure. Other people find the thrilling excitement of continuing discovery. They have a wide frontier and keep pushing into it. Married life is always charged with adventure. There is always something new and interesting. Life has not enough time for all of its eager enterprises and not enough room for all its wonders.

Happy is the couple who feel the tingling sense not only of discovering life, but of a growing discovery of each other. Their hearts become more and more intertwined as they push back the edgeless horizon until the closing of life's day. They may have occupied a cottage or a mansion, a tiny town lot or a wide field, but they have filled it full of living and of themselves. It is a long way from the new-lit candle at the marriage altar to the guttering, flickering blaze of a candle's spent stub, but the light is the same and the loveliness is the same, and the glow is the same. What loveliness it has revealed and seen as it has given itself **away to** push back the darkness!

Those who cultivate orchids have a dull task compared with those who culture a marriage, for the flowering of a marriage is the loveliest and most fragrant product of our human endeavor. A well-cultured marriage blossoms continually and fills its environs with the heady fragrance of love. But only those who carefully keep back the pests, trim the branches, and water the roots will enjoy the full spreading loveliness of it. The finest marriages don't just happen; they're cultured.